nitty gritty books

Seafoods Cookbook	Soups & Stews	To My Daughter, With Love
Quick Breads	Crepes & Omelets	Natural Foods
Pasta & Rice	Microwave Cooking	Chinese Vegetarian
Calorie Watchers Cookbook	Vegetable Cookbook	The Jewish Cookbook
Pies & Cakes	Kid's Arts and Crafts	Working Couples
Yogurt	Bread Baking	Mexican
The Ground Beef Cookbook	The Crockery Pot Cookbook	Sunday Breakfast
Cocktails & Hors d'Oeuvres	Kid's Garden Book	Fisherman's Wharf Cookbook
Casseroles & Salads	Classic Greek Cooking	Barbecue Cookbook
Kid's Party Book	Low Carbohydrate Cookbook	Ice Cream Cookbook
Pressure Cooking	Kid's Cookbook	Blender Cookbook
Food Processor Cookbook	Italian	The Wok, a Chinese Cookbook
Peanuts & Popcorn	Cheese Guide & Cookbook	Japanese Country
Kid's Pets Book	Miller's German	Fondue Cookbook
Make It Ahead French Cooking	Quiche & Souffle	

designed with giving in mind

To **PAMELA KAUFMAN** and to **PENNY SCHMITTER** — those "skinny" girls who least needed my cooking and yet, most enjoyed it. Thank you for all your encouragement. My deepest gratitude to **DR. ABRAHAM KAUFMAN**, my "medical" gourmet!

CALORIE WATCHERS

COOKBOOK

by
Annouk Mamalis-van de Voorde

Illustrated by Mike Nelson

A Nitty Gritty Book*
Published by
Nitty Gritty Productions
P.O. Box 5457
Concord, California 94524

*Nitty Gritty Books — Trademark
Owned by Nitty Gritty Productions
Concord, California

ISBN 0-911954-50-3
Library of Congress Catalog Card Number: 78-74603

TABLE OF CONTENTS

INTRODUCTION

Within the last few years, America has become diet conscious. Most of us are now calorie watchers. Some of us only casually. Others go so far as to count each calorie. Still others join one of the sensible programs that automatically does the "watching" for them.

That's how thousands of former fatties, including myself, have become slim.

I joined an organization which helped me to achieve my weight goal. But, after eating bland meats and mounds of plain vegetables for what seemed like an eternity, I thought to myself, "There has to be a better way." I decided to create some new and exciting diet recipes by drawing on my cultural heritage and world wide travel experience. I wanted to make these recipes tasty enough for even non-dieters to relish.

Throughout my life I have been exposed to many different cultures. I was raised in the Belgian Congo, now Zaire. My father, who traveled frequently, told me mouthwatering tales of meals in foreign lands. My mother was the best French cook I have ever met. She loved to plan and prepare elegant dinner parties. From my grandfather I learned the joys of native Russian cusine. When I became older, I began traveling to South Africa, Western Europe and the United States. My husband, Greek by birth, introduced me to a thousand and one Near and Middle Eastern foods.

My struggle with weight began at an early age. When I was living in Africa with my parents, I was 35 pounds overweight. I dragged my heavily padded body from doctor to doctor, demanding pills, diets and instant solutions. For nearly 10 years I went through the dieter's "yo-yo syndrome." For two weeks I would lose a few pounds. Within another couple weeks I'd be right back where I started from, maybe even plus a pound or two! Sometimes I would starve myself until I was almost faint. By the time I reached America and got married, I was slightly overweight, but the temptations of American food were just too much.

Just as I was about to reach the end of my rope, a friend introduced me to an organization which had been successful in "re-educating" people about their eating habits. I didn't have to count my calories. Their recipes did that for me. To my surprise, the portions were big enough to feed a truckdriver. Shortly thereafter, I lost a lot of weight. I was down to a size 10!

But even roses have thorns. The plentitude was boring. Eating wasn't exciting, only dull. I craved fascinating foods. Using the techniques I learned in my weight control classes, and the vast cultural experience I had gained while growing up, I began to create "slimmed down" recipes I have enjoyed all my life. Such favorites as Pizza, Moussaka and sauce-smothered French classics were among the first I experimented with. No more carrot sticks or cottage cheese for me!

Over the years, I have continued to test and retest my recipes. Even people who don't have to watch their weight like them. Many of my non-dieting friends have made such comments as, "How can you stay so slim, eating all these rich foods?" My daughter Tania prefers my version of Crepes Suzette to the taditional, because she says, "It tastes richer." These recipes are ones which your whole family will enjoy, whether they are dieters or not.

For those of you who are very serious about a weight-loss program, I have written many recipes for one serving only. Dieting is often a lonely business. You may, however, simply double, triple or quadruple these recipes to serve your whole family. There is no need to violate your diet if you are planning a party. Just increase a recipe from this book to serve as many guests as you plan on inviting.

Not only do I include many international delicacies, I also give you instructions on how to "de-calorize" your favorite recipes.

Best wishes for getting and staying slim.

INGREDIENTS

Very few special ingredients and no special equipment are used in my recipes. That's the whole point of this book — you cook and eat normally. However, I do urge you to invest in a really good (and that often means expensive) non-stick skillet. This one utensil, along with the following easy-to-buy ingredients will help you get the best results.

BACON BITS — Imitation bacon bits, usually sold in jars or shakers, are a substitute for real bacon. They have a satisfying flavor and fewer calories.

BREAD — for thickening sauces. I use the popular-program method of substituting a slice of bread for flour. Bread thickens sauces easily, without lumping, as flour can. Also, those on certain programs can more easily count their bread allowances. Many programs permit arrowroot, available in jars at spice counters, for thickening; 2 teaspoons of arrowroot can be used instead of 1 slice of bread in sauce recipes.

BREAD CRUMBS — Toast bread and let dry a bit. Break into blender container and whirl to fineness desired.

CHEESE — Cottage cheese, Italian ricotta cheese and farmer's cheese (the "pot" type resembling cottage cheese) are interchangeable. I prefer the flavor and texture of ricotta.

CHICKEN SEASONING — Many recipes call for "chicken seasoning." You have the following three choices:

5

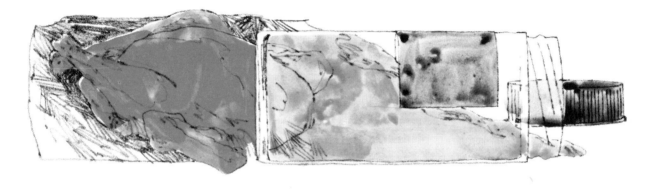

1. Chicken stock base, a light yellow powder in jars at spice sections (measure amount recipe calls for).

2. Chicken-flavored instant broth and seasoning, a light yellow powder in little envelopes (use 1 envelope for each teaspoon "chicken seasoning" called for in my recipes).

3. Instant chicken bouillon, a golden-brown granular powder in jars where bouillon cubes are sold (measure amount recipe calls for).

6

CHIVES — The measurement in my recipes is for fresh chopped chives. You can substitute the freeze-dried kind sold in bottles at spice counters. Use half as much dried as fresh. You may also substitute very finely minced green onion tops.

MAYONNAISE — Imitation mayonnaise, labeled as such on the jar, so much resembles richer real mayonnaise that you may not be able to tell the difference except in your slimmer figure.

MEAT — Much of the fat in chicken is in the skin, so my recipes call for removing the skin. Most red meats contain quite a bit of visible and invisible fat. My recipes remove as much of this fat as possible.

MILK — Liquid nonfat milk is meant when a recipe specifies "nonfat milk." Use dry nonfat milk powder (don't mix with water) when the recipe calls for "instant nonfat dry milk."

OILS AND FATS — All fats contain approximately the same calories — about 100 per tablespoon — whether they are butter, margarine, vegetable oils, meat or even fish fats. My recipes "get the fat out" every possible way. However, because just the sight of golden butter sets our mouths awatering and just a taste satisfies, I use a very small amount to top certain dishes. If you want to cut calories still further, omit butter (or oil) added as a topping.

tain dishes. If you want to cut calorie count still further, omit butter (or oil) added as a topping.

ONION POWDER—An onion flavored seasoning in a jar at spice sections; or you might use a small envelope labeled "onion-flavored instant broth and seasoning."

PARSLEY—The measurements in my recipes are for fresh parsley, but often you can substitute the dried kind available in jars at spice counters. Use a third as much dried as fresh; for example, use 1 teaspoon dried for 1 tablespoon (equal to 3 teaspoons) fresh minced parsley.

RICE—Several of my recipes call for 1/2 cup cooked rice. Many other dishes, particularly those with sauce, are best served with cooked rice. To prepare 1/2 cup successfully, use the following method:

Into a small nonstick saucepan, put 1/2 cup water, 1/8 teaspoon salt and 3 level tablespoons regular long-grain white rice. Bring to a boil, cover and immediately reduce heat to lowest possible; cook 15 minutes. Yield: 1/2 cup. Calories: 100.

SEASAME OIL—The kind to use is golden brown, with a very intense flavor and aroma. Usually you must buy it at Oriental, health food or gourmet stores. A very few drops give food a marvelous richness. The light gold, refined sesame salad oil doesn't have the same qualities.

SUGAR SUBSTITUTES—If you don't like these, use 1 or 2 teaspoons honey or sugar for each little envelope of sugar substitute.

TOMATO SAUCE—Use the canned sauce that does not contain oil or added sweeteners. Tomato puree, if available, is of almost the same thickness and may be substituted. I do not recommend the thicker tomato paste (even if thinned with water to sauce consistency) because it has a different flavor.

APPITIZERS & BEVERAGES

The "happy" hour can be the most painful one for a dieter. We are denied cocktails and must resist tempting rich hors d'oeuvres. Still, there are choices we can make that will allow us to satisfy the urge to nibble while we sip, yet not add to our total calorie count too outrageously.

The recipes that follow will help. When you need some impromptu ideas, try these:

When in season, luscious ripe strawberries on crushed ice, au naturel, will make a bright and tasty addition to cocktail time. Accompany with a crystal bowl of yogurt flavored with a touch of almond extract and some sugar substitute.

Another trick: fill a bowl with partially frozen melon balls, dusted with ginger and speared with toothpicks. Super low "cal."

Last, but not least, always have a dish of crudites, fresh raw vegetables, to be eaten out of hand. Try cauliflowerets, stringbeans, mushrooms, cherry tomatoes and celery stuffed with yogurt and chives. The more colorful the combination, the better.

HUMMUS (GARBANZO DIP) All the Middle East

This dip is popular in Greece, Turkey, the Arab countries and Israel. Accompany with raw vegetables or a sensible amount of round, hollow Middle Eastern pita (pocket) bread, sold in many American markets.

1/2 cup canned garbanzos or chick peas, drained (save juice)
2 tsp. sesame oil (optional, see introduction)
2 tbs. lemon juice
1 clove garlic
salt, paprika, cayenne
fresh chopped parsley for garnish (optional)

To blender container add about 2 tablespoons garbanzo juice, oil, lemon juice and garlic. Blend until garlic is pureed. Add beans and blend until smooth, using more juice if necessary. Mixture should be thick. Season with salt and more lemon juice to taste. Sprinkle with paprika and cayenne, if desired. Add a rim of parsley. Serve at room temperature. (Dip may be made as much as a day ahead if refrigerated.) Makes 1 serving.

Calories: 190 per serving

BOURSIN (SPICED CHEESE)

The French flavor cheese by coating with herbs, leaves, even grape seeds. Here black pepper bits enfuse every bite with aroma and exotica. Serve with crisp vegetable dippers.

2/3 cup (6 ozs.) ricotta or cottage cheese
1/4 tsp. (or more) garlic powder
1 tbs. chopped chives
1/2 tsp. onion powder
2 tsp. minced parsley

1/3 cup instant nonfat dry milk
1/8 tsp. crumbled thyme
2 tbs. imitation mayonnaise
salt
very coarsely ground or cracked pepper

With rotary mixer, beat cheese until smooth. Stir in remaining ingredients except salt and coarsely ground pepper. Add salt to taste. Chill until firm. Form into patty. Roll all over in coarse pepper. Wrap and chill several hours, preferably overnight, for flavor to develop. Makes 2 appetizer servings.

Calories: 185 per serving

ROQUEFORT PIE MOUSSE

An elegant beginning to a special dinner party . . . and you can prepare it a day ahead.

1/2 cup skim evaporated milk
1 env. unflavored gelatin
3-1/2 ozs. Danish Havarti cheese or Swiss (about 1 cup shredded)
2-1/2 ozs. Roquefort cheese, crumbled
1 tsp. Worchestershire sauce
1 tbs. fresh parsley, minced
1/4 tsp. garlic powder
freshly ground pepper to taste
pinch nutmeg

Put milk in mixing bowl and set in freezer, along with beaters from mixer for about 45 minutes. Meanwhile, into a small saucepan put gelatin and 1/4 cup cold water; soften gelatin and cook on low heat just until gelatin dissolves; remove. In medium sized skillet bring 1/2 cup water to boil. Place Havarti and Roquefort in a smaller skillet. Set smaller skillet in the boiling water and let cheese soften. Do not melt completely. Remove small skillet from water and add remaining ingredients to cheeses. Mix evenly. Refrigerate cheese mixture and dissolved gelatin separately. When gelatin starts barely mounding (looks like slightly beaten egg whites, but do not let it gel) remove evaporated milk from freezer. With frozen beaters, whip milk until stiff peaks form; beat in gelatin and cheese mixture at the same time. Pour mixture into 8-inch pie plate or 3-4 cup mold and refrigerate until firm. This might take several hours. Unmold mousse, by dipping bottom of pie plate in one inch warm water a few seconds. Hold serving platter on top and invert. Surround with thin rye bread or crackers. Serve chilled. Makes three servings.

1 Saltine cracker.
Calories: 223 per serving (without bread).

CAVIAR PIE

Lumpfish caviar, the most inexpensive form of black caviar, can be found in little jars in gourmet sections of many supermarkets and department stores.

2/3 cup (6 ozs.) ricotta or cottage cheese
3 tbs. lemon juice
1 tsp. chicken seasoning (see page 6)
1 tbs. (1/2 oz.) minced onion
4 hard-cooked eggs, grated

2 tsp. imitation mayonnaise
3-1/2 ozs. lumpfish caviar, well drained
minced fresh parsley for garnish
crackers or melba toast

In bowl, beat cheese, lemon juice, chicken seasoning and onion with wooden spoon until smooth; chill about 30 minutes, or until firm enough to spread. Meanwhile, mix eggs with mayonnaise. On serving platter, shape into patty about 1 inch thick. Chill. Using spatula, smooth caviar firmly onto top of egg patty. Carefully spread cheese over patty to mask top and edges. Garnish with parsley. Serve well chilled with crackers. Makes 4 appetizer servings.

One 4" x 4" Melba toast: 39 calories
Calories: 255 per serving (without crackers)

CHILE BEAN DIP

Four forms of the chile pepper season this dip. Carrot sticks and celery would be compatible fresh dippers; so would slices of raw jicama, a brown-skinned Mexican root vegetable that is white, crisp and sweet after being peeled.

1/3 cup (3 ozs.) cottage or ricotta cheese
1 cup cooked red kidney beans, drained
1 jar (4 ozs.) pimientos, drained (save juice)
1/2 tsp. crushed red pepper
1 small hot canned chile (optional)
3 cloves garlic, minced
1/4 cup tomato sauce
1 tsp. chili powder
salt and lemon juice (optional)

Combine all ingredients except salt and lemon juice in blender container in order listed. Blend until smooth, adding pimiento juice if necessary. Season with salt and lemon juice as desired. Makes 2 appetizer servings.

18

Calories: 182 per serving

TURNIPS LEBANESE

Lightly pickled vegetables from an exotic part of the world—a great appetizer change from plain old carrot sticks and other such boring fare.

1 lb. raw turnips
red wine vinegar
2 tsp. salt
4 tsp. olive oil

Peel and cut turnips into sticks of very thin French-fry size. Arrange in single layer in large glass dish. Cover with vinegar to measure proper amount, then drain vinegar into saucepan and bring to boil (this reduces tartness). Rearrange turnips and sprinkle evenly with salt. Cover with boiled vinegar. Marinate covered in refrigerator several days, turning occasionally. Drain and eat cold, drizzled with oil. Makes 4 appetizer servings.

EGGPLANT A LA GREQUE

Often called eggplant salad, this versatile dip for breadsticks or French bread also traditionally is served on individual plates as an appetizer, side dish or salad course.

2 medium eggplants
juice of about 2 lemons
8 cloves garlic, pureed
1/4 cup yogurt or buttermilk
1 tsp. crumbled oregano
1/4 tsp. crumbled basil

1 tsp. dried dill weed
   or 1 tbs. chopped fresh dill
1/4 cup olive oil
salt and pepper
parsley or lemon slices for garnish

Arrange unpeeled eggplants on broiler rack. Place close to preheated broiler, turning often so that peel chars all over. Place in colander over bowl. When cool enough to handle, remove peel and seeds; discard. In bowl, chop pulp, adding lemon juice to prevent darkening; then mash completely with fork as you blend in the garlic, yogurt, oregano, basil, dill and oil. (Blender can also be used.) Season with salt and pepper. Serve at room temperature with garnish. (Make ahead several hours or even refrigerate overnight.) Makes 4 appetizer servings.

Calories: 175 per serving

ARTICHOKES VINAIGRETTE

4 medium artichokes
8 tbs. imitation mayonnaise
3 tbs. white vinegar
4 tbs. chopped chives
2 cloves garlic, minced

4 tbs. fresh lemon juice
1-1/2 tsp. oregano leaves, crushed
salt and freshly ground pepper
1 tsp. prepared mustard

Wash artichokes under plenty of running water. Using scissors or a sharp knife, cut off tips. Cut stem off flush with the base. Drop prepared artichokes into boiling salted water to cover. Simmer, covered, until outer leaves pull off easily, about 40 minutes. Or cook in a pressure cooker with 1 cup boiling water for 12 minutes from the time control jiggles. Remove artichokes from water and turn upside down to drain. Keep warm. Combine remaining ingredients. Divide evenly into four small individual dishes. Arrange artichokes on individual plates accompanied by the sauce dishes. To eat, remove leaves one at a time and dip the meaty part at the base of the leaf into sauce and scrape off between your teeth. Enjoy the heart of the artichoke as well as the stem but do not forget to remove the fuzzy portion which is not edible. Makes 4 servings.

Calories: 180 per serving

PINA COLADA

Serious calorie watchers who avoid the high count of alcohol will happily sip just one of these tall beautiful drinks throughout the whole happy hour.

1/2 cup canned crushed pineapple in its own juice, frozen solid
3/4 cup nonfat milk or 1/2 cup evaporated nonfat milk
1/4 tsp. coconut flavoring
1 to 2 envs. sugar substitute
pinch each nutmeg and ginger
1/4 tsp. (or more) rum flavoring

In blender jar, combine all ingredients. Blend at high speed until just creamy and foamy. Pour into tall, slim tumbler. Sprinkle foam with a delicate pinch of nutmeg. Makes 1 serving.

Calories: 105 per serving

YOGURT COOLER

Thinned yogurt is made into refreshing drinks in all the countries where yogurt is everyday fare. The rosewater used in the Indian version is not essential, but can be found more easily than you may expect at gourmet departments of supermarkets and department stores, as well as in Greek and Middle Eastern shops.

1/2 cup yogurt thinned with 1/2 cup water
1 env. sugar substitute
1/2 tsp. rosewater
1 drop red food coloring (optional)
4 ice cubes, cracked
crumbled dried mint or minced fresh mint

In blender jar, combine all ingredients except mint. Blend just until ice is crushed. Pour into tall glass, top with mint, insert straws. Makes 1 serving.

Calories: 75 per serving

SOUPS

When you think temptation is going to get the best of you, it's time for soup. Many an incurable nibbler, like me, has found soups to be a salvation. They are just what I need to make it between meals without "cheating." Deliciously hot during the winter months, they fill my cold and empty stomach. When served chilled in the summer, they are refreshing and totally satisfying.

Happily, many soups have few calories. Almost any little foil covered dish in your refrigerator harbors the possibility of soup. Leftover vegetables come alive when a little skim milk and a few spices are added to them

Here is the perfect opportunity to put your new food processor to work. If you don't have one, a blender will do the trick almost as nicely.

Here is the opportunity to put that new food processor to use, but of course, a blender will do just fine.

If you are a calorie watcher, don't forget soups!

CREAM OF WATERCRESS SOUP

Creme de Cresson, in its native land. An all-weather soup to serve hot or cold.

2 bunches watercress
1 stalk celery
1/2 tsp. onion powder
1 cup nonfat milk
1 cup (6 ozs.) diced cooked potato
2 tbs. butter or margarine
salt and freshly ground pepper
pinch of dill weed
parsley sprig for garnish

To saucepan, add watercress, celery, 1/4 teaspoon onion powder and 1 cup water. Cover and simmer just until watercress is wilted but still bright green. Pour into blender jar; add milk, potato and butter. Blend until smooth. Season with salt and pepper. Serve hot or cold, dusted with dill and garnished with parsley. Makes 2 servings.

Calories: 200 per serving

CREAM OF SPINACH SOUP

Two of the most vitamin-packed green vegetables are combined in this soup that is delicious hot or chilled.

1 large bunch parsley
1 cup cooked spinach, well drained
salt
1/8 tsp. nutmeg
2 tbs. lemon juice

1 chicken bouillon cube
1/4 tsp. onion powder
1 tbs. butter or margarine
5 small fresh mint leaves or 1/4 tsp. dried mint
1/2 to 3/4 cup buttermilk or nonfat milk

Discard parsley stems, chop and put in saucepan with 1/4 cup water and dash of salt. Simmer until soft, but still bright green. Drain well. In blender jar, combine all ingredients, starting with 1/2 cup milk only. Blend until smooth. Add remaining milk if you want a thinner soup. Serve hot or cold. Makes 1 serving.

Calories: 230 per serving

VELOUTE DE POIS

It would scarcely do this soup justice to call it cream of pea. An elegant first course, served very cold.

1-1/2 cups (10 ozs.) fresh or frozen peas
1/4 head iceberg lettuce (or 1 heart), chopped
2/3 cup (4 ozs.) chopped onion
2 chicken bouillon cubes
several sprigs fresh parsley or 1 tsp. dried parsley
salt and freshly ground pepper
1 cup buttermilk
4 tsp. butter or margarine
8 leaves mint, chopped, or 1/4 tsp. crumbled dried mint

In saucepan, combine peas, lettuce, onion, bouillon cubes and 1/4 to 1/2 cup water. Cover and simmer until peas are tender but still bright green. Pour into blender jar, add parsley and blend until smooth. Pour into saucepan, add salt and pepper, buttermilk and butter; heat. Pour into serving bowls, sprinkle with mint and chill. Makes 4 servings.

Calories: 117 per serving

CREAM OF MUSHROOM SOUP

Creamy but not caloric.

1 cup (3 ozs.) sliced fresh mushrooms
1 chicken bouillon cube
1/4 tsp. onion powder
1 tbs. minced parsley or 1 tsp. dried parsley
salt and freshly ground pepper
pinch nutmeg
1/2 cup nonfat milk
1/2 tsp. fresh chopped dill or pinch dried dill weed
1 tsp. butter or margarine

To saucepan, add mushrooms, bouillon cube, onion powder, parsley and 1 cup water. Simmer uncovered until liquid is reduced to 1/2 cup. Pour into blender jar, add salt, pepper and nutmeg and blend until creamy. Return to pan, add milk and heat to serving temperature. Serve sprinkled with dill and topped with butter. Makes 1 serving.

Calories: 118 per serving

POTAGE JULIENNE France

Once you start making soups like this, you will never go back to opening cans.

1 small (2 ozs.) carrot
1 small (2 ozs.) raw beet
1 medium (2 ozs.) parsnip
1/2 medium (2 ozs.) onion
1 small (2 ozs.) leek (white part only)
3 chicken bouillon cubes
salt and freshly ground pepper

4 or 5 lettuce or escarole leaves, chopped
1/2 cup (2 ozs.) fresh or frozen peas
pinch sugar
1-1/2 tsp. dill weed
1 tbs. butter or margarine
1-1/2 tsp. Maggi seasoning (optional)

Peel carrot, beet and parsnip. Cut them into thin strips. Cut onion into thin rings and chop leek. Put vegetables into kettle and add bouillon cubes, salt, pepper and 6 cups water. Cover, bring to boil, lower heat and simmer until vegetables are almost tender. Add lettuce, peas and sugar. Simmer uncovered 5 minutes or until liquid is somewhat reduced and peas are tender. Serve hot, sprinkled with dill and dotted with butter. Add Maggi seasoning, if desired. Makes 3 main-dish servings.

Calories: 96 per serving

VICHYSSOISE

Serve ice cold and dust delicately with dill. Looks dazzling in long stemmed glasses. .

1 medium (about 3 ozs.) potato, cut up
2 ozs. chopped onion
2 ozs. chopped leek
1 cup water
1 tsp. chicken seasoning (see page 6)
salt and freshly ground pepper

1 tbs. minced parsley
1 tbs. butter or margarine
pinch dillweed
1/4 cup thick buttermilk
1/2 cup skim milk

In medium skillet, combine first five ingredients. Cover skillet and cook slowly about 12 minutes or until vegetables are tender and liquid somewhat reduced. Add salt, pepper, butter and dillweed. Pour into blender jar and blend until creamy. Stir in milks. Refrigerate. Makes one serving.

Calories: 310 per serving

CUCUMBER SOUP

An almost invisible dent in your calorie count for the day.

4 medium cucumbers, peeled
2-3 (4 ozs.) chopped leeks (white part only)
salt and pepper, preferably white pepper
2 slices white bread
nutmeg
about 6 sprigs fresh parsley or 2 tsp. dried parsley
2 tsp. white vinegar or lemon juice
garnish: thin slices of cucumber, parsley or dill sprigs

Cut cucumbers lengthwise into sticks; remove seeds and cut into bite-sized chunks. Put in saucepan and cover with water, add leeks, salt and pepper. Simmer covered for 15-20 minutes. Remove vegetables with slotted spoon and keep warm. Pour liquid remaining into blender jar, add bread, dash nutmeg and parsley. Blend until smooth. Pour into small skillet over medium heat and cook, stirring, until thickened. Add warm vegetables, vinegar, salt and pepper as needed. Serve warm with garnish. Makes 4 servings.

Calories: 70 per serving.

COLD BORSCH

Quick to make if you use canned vegetables.

1/2 cup (3 ozs.) cooked sliced beets, drained
3 tbs. beet juice
1/4 cup (1 oz.) cooked sliced carrots, drained
1/4 cup tomato sauce
1/4 cup buttermilk
1/4 tsp. onion powder
1 beef bouillon cube
2 tbs. lemon juice
salt and freshly ground pepper
garnish: dill weed and fresh or dried mint

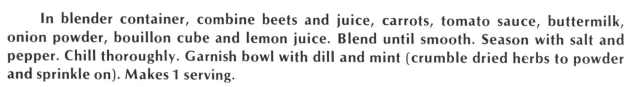

In blender container, combine beets and juice, carrots, tomato sauce, buttermilk, onion powder, bouillon cube and lemon juice. Blend until smooth. Season with salt and pepper. Chill thoroughly. Garnish bowl with dill and mint (crumble dried herbs to powder and sprinkle on). Makes 1 serving.

34   Calories: 109 per serving

GAZPACHO

Is cold Gazpacho a soupy salad or a salad-like soup? Either one, depending on your mood.

4 medium tomatoes, peeled
4 cloves garlic
1 medium (5 ozs.) onion
1 tsp. chicken bouillon or onion powder
salt and freshly ground pepper
1 medium cucumber, diced
1 sweet red bell pepper, diced
1 medium green bell pepper, diced
4 slices whole wheat bread, toasted and cut in cubes

In blender jar, combine tomatoes, garlic, onion and bouillon. Blend until smooth, adding water if necessary. Mixture should be thick. Season with salt and pepper. Pour into soup bowls and chill thoroughly. At serving time, top with equal amounts of the cucumber, bell peppers, and bread cubes. Makes 4 servings.

Calories: 116 per serving

CONSOMME MADRILENE EN GELEE

A beautiful treat for guests or yourself. Show off the lovely color in glass bowls or over-size wine goblets.

1-1/2 envs. unflavored gelatin	juice of 2 limes
2 cups tomato juice	salt and freshly ground pepper
1/2 tsp. Worcestershire sauce	about 7 ice cubes, cracked
2 beef bouillon cubes	grated rind of 1 lime
1/4 tsp. onion powder	parsley sprigs or 1 tsp. black caviar
2 tsp. wine vinegar	

Soften gelatin in tomato juice. Pour into saucepan over low heat and stir constantly to dissolve gelatin. Add Worcestershire, bouillon cubes, onion powder, vinegar, lime juice; heat just until cubes dissolve; taste and add salt and pepper. Pour into bowl and chill until set. Put mixture into blender jar and blend, adding an ice cube at a time, until doubled in volume and a pale pink color. Serve in glass bowls, sherbet glasses or goblets. Garnish with lime rind and parsley or caviar. Makes 3 servings.

Calories: 85 per serving

ONION SOUP AU GRATIN

Satisfying, hot and simple to prepare.

1-1/2 cups water
1 medium (4 ozs.) thinly sliced onion
1/2 tsp. onion powder
1 beef bouillon cube
salt and freshly ground pepper
1 slice whole wheat bread, toasted until crisp
about 1/2 cup (1-1/2 ozs.) Swiss cheese, shredded
2 tbs. (1/2 oz.) grated Parmesan cheese

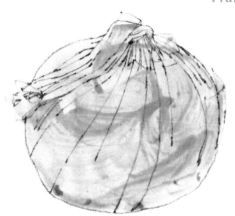

Pour water into medium sized skillet. Bring to a boil. Add onion, onion powder, bouillon cube, salt and pepper and stir to dissolve. Pour the soup into an earthenware, ovenproof soup bowl or ramekin. Slightly immerse toasted bread on top of the soup. Place Swiss cheese on toast. Cover top of soup with Parmesan; add more freshly ground pepper if desired. Place dish in preheated 350°F. oven. Bake 10 minutes, until top is browned and cheese bubbly. Makes 1 serving.

Calories: 321 per serving

OYSTER SOUP WITH CROUTONS

This French version of oyster stew has style and chic worthy of "the Beautiful People," or of those who will be beautiful after they shed a pound or two.

2 slices white bread
powdered thyme and garlic powder
12 ozs. canned or fresh oysters with juices
3 stalks celery, finely chopped
2 small cloves garlic, minced
1 cup nonfat milk

1 chicken bouillon cube
1/4 tsp. each, onion powder
   and crumbled tarragon
1 tbs. minced parsley or 1 tsp. dried parsley
salt and pepper, preferably white pepper
2 thin slices lime or lemon for garnish

First make croutons: Cut bread in cubes, dust lightly with thyme and garlic powder, place on baking sheet in 300⁰F. oven and bake just until beginning to brown. Reserve. To saucepan, add oyster juice, celery and garlic; simmer, adding water as necessary, until celery is tender but firm. Add oysters, milk, bouillon cube, onion powder, tarragon, parsley and half of the croutons. Heat very slowly, stirring (do not let simmer); add salt and pepper. Pour into serving bowls, top with remaining croutons and citrus slices. Makes 2 supper servings.

Calories: 276 per serving

NEW ENGLAND CLAM CHOWDER

A total meal, extra rich and creamy . . . yet extra stingy on calories!

1 cup water
1 tsp. chicken seasoning (see page 6)
2 ozs. chopped scallions
1 medium (about 3 ozs.) potato, diced
2 ozs. diced carrot
2 tsp. diet margarine
2 tsp. arrowroot

3/4 cup skim milk
4 ozs. minced canned clams, drained
1/2 cup clam juice
salt and freshly ground pepper
minced fresh parsley
pinch nutmeg
1 tsp. butter or margarine

In medium skillet, combine water, chicken seasoning, scallions, potato and carrot. Bring to a boil. Simmer until vegetables are tender, about 15 minutes. Reserve vegetables and 1/2 cup pan juice. In small skillet melt margarine and sprinkle with arrowroot to make a paste. Over medium heat add milk slowly, stirring constantly until smooth and thickened. Add reserved vegetables and juice, clams, clam juice, salt and pepper. Cook, stirring, another two minutes. Serve piping hot garnished with parsley and nutmeg. Drizzle with butter. Makes one luncheon or dinner serving.

Calories: 398 per serving

NEW YORK CLAM CHOWDER

This is a Manhattan-style tomato chowder, for the very hungry!

6 oz. canned clams with juice
1/2 cup (3 ozs.) diced carrots
1/4 cup (1 oz.) coarsely chopped onion
1-1/2 stalks celery, chopped
1 chicken bouillon cube
1-1/2 cups tomato juice

1/2 cup fresh green beans, cut in pieces
1 medium yellow summer squash, cut in pieces
3 tbs. chopped parsley or 1 tbs. dried
Worcestershire sauce to taste
salt and freshly ground pepper
1 tbs. salad oil

Into saucepan, put clam juice, carrots, onion, celery, bouillon cube and 1/4 cup water. Cover and simmer 15 minutes, adding water if necessary, just until vegetables are tender and liquid is absorbed. Add tomato juice, beans and squash. Cover and simmer for 15 minutes, or until beans are tender but firm. Add clams, parsley, Worcestershire, salt and lots of pepper. Heat and serve, drizzled with oil. Makes 1 main-dish serving.

Calories: 423 per serving

CHICKEN-RICE SOUP AVGOLEMONO

4 ozs. uncooked chicken thigh or
    drumstick, skin removed
1 chicken bouillon cube
1/4 cup (1 oz.) sliced carrot
6 very thin slices onion (1 oz.)
1 stalk celery, finely diced
1 tbs. chopped parsley

1/4 tsp. crumbled oregano
1 clove garlic, minced
salt
3 tbs. uncooked rice
1 large egg, separated
juice of 1 lemon
2 tsp. butter or margarine

Into saucepan, put chicken, 2 cups water, bouillon, carrot, onion, celery, parsley, oregano, garlic and 1/4 teaspoon salt. Cover and simmer for 15 minutes; add rice. Cover and cook about 15-20 minutes more, or until chicken is tender, adding pepper and more salt if necessary. Remove chicken, discard bones, shred and return to soup. Increase heat and cook broth uncovered until reduced to about 1 cup liquid. Just before serving, beat egg white until very stiff, beat in yolk and then lemon juice. Pour egg mixture on top of warm soup. Heat (do not let simmer or egg will curdle), just until hot and slightly thickened. Serve dotted with butter. Makes 1 serving.

Calories: 452 per serving

MAIN DISH SALADS

Every dieter wants to make "less" look and taste like "more." These main dish salads are designed to do just that.

I have often served my Pineapple-Coconut Chicken to dinner guests. When I tell them that the beautiful and delicious dish they just consumed was low in calories, they don't believe me.

The main ingredients in salads are greens. Therefore, their quality and freshness is essential. Always wash greens carefully and pat them dry with paper towels. Store them in the refrigerator, wrapped in damp paper towels, until you need them.

My salads aren't just lettuce with low calorie dressing, they are eye pleasing delicacies which are suitable for light lunches or suppers. They are nutritious and low in calories. A bargain—yes?

GREEK SALAD

This attractive salad looks best in a glass bowl as either a main dish or salad course.

1 garlic clove
2-3 Salonica peppers (in brine) or 1 large dill pickle, finely chopped
4 tsp. olive oil
4 tsp. wine vinegar, preferably tarragon
1/2 medium tomato
romaine, chicory or curly endive and iceberg lettuce, torn in pieces
1/2 unpeeled cucumber, thinly sliced
1/3 cup (2 ozs.) diced feta cheese
3/4 cup (4 ozs.) finely chopped green onions
several pinches crumbled oregano
1/4 tsp. crumbled basil or mint
salt and freshly ground pepper
2 hard-cooked eggs, cut in wedges

Rub serving bowl with cut garlic and set bowl aside. Then mince garlic and combine in

44

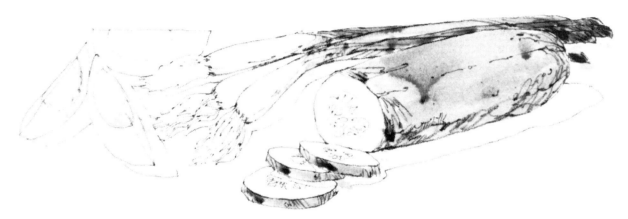

small bowl with peppers, olive oil and vinegar. Hold tomato over bowl to catch juice as you cut it into small pieces. Add tomato to pepper mixture and stir to combine ingredients. In large mixing bowl combine greens, cucumber, cheese, onions, oregano and basil. Chill. At serving time add salt, pepper and dressing. Lightly toss and transfer to serving bowl. Garnish with eggs. Makes 2 main-dish or 4 dinner-salad servings.

Calories: 303 or 151 per serving

TOSSED SALAD NICOISE French-inspired

Do you dare not to be authentic? Traditional Nicoise has oil-rich dressing, olives and many more calories than this one. The results of this lighter combination are worth the risk.

1-1/4 cups diced potato (7 ozs.)
2 cups fresh green beans cut in 1/2-inch pieces
2 firm tomatoes, cut in wedges
2 tbs. drained capers
2 cloves garlic, minced
romaine or leaf lettuce, torn in pieces
1/4 cup (3 ozs.) red onion, thinly sliced

8 ozs. tuna, well drained
salt and freshly ground pepper
1 tsp. Dijon mustard
1/2 tsp. crumbled chervil
1/4 tsp. crumbled tarragon
1 tbs. wine vinegar
2 tbs. olive oil

Cook potatoes and green beans separately until barely tender. Chill. Set aside a few tomato wedges and capers for garnish. Rub salad bowl with some of the garlic. Add lettuce, onion, tuna, potatoes, beans, tomatoes, capers, salt and pepper. Stir together remaining ingredients; pour over salad and toss. Makes 2 main-dish salads.

Calories: 501 per serving

SEAFOOD SALAD

A pretty main-dish salad that can be made hours ahead of time.

1/2 cup cooked rice (see page 9)
4 ozs. tuna or crabmeat, drained
2 tbs. imitation mayonnaise
1 tbs. lemon juice
1 tsp. chicken seasoning (see page 6)
1/4 tsp. each onion powder and ground cumin
1 tsp. (or more) curry powder
freshly ground pepper
salad greens
1 tomato and pimiento strips for garnish

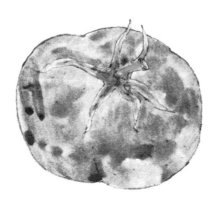

In mixing bowl, combine rice, tuna, mayonnaise, lemon juice and seasonings. Mix well. Pack into small mold or bowl. Cover and chill several hours. Unmold onto bed of greens and garnish with tomato wedges and pimiento. Makes 1 serving.

Calories: 469 per serving

CRAB IN ASPIC

Although you can easily increase the ingredients to serve many guests, you can quickly prepare this glamorous molded salad to pamper yourself — you're worth it.

1 env. unflavored gelatin
1/2 cup buttermilk or yogurt
1 tsp. chicken seasoning (see page 6)
1/4 tsp. onion powder
2 tbs. imitation mayonnaise
1 tbs. tarragon vinegar
grated peel and juice of 1 lime
3 ice cubes, cracked
1 can (6 ozs.) crabmeat
2 medium dill pickles, chopped
salt and freshly ground pepper
lettuce leaves, pimiento strips and radishes for garnish

Soften gelatin in 1/4 cup cold water. Mix with buttermilk, chicken seasoning and onion powder in small saucepan. Cook over low heat, stirring, until gelatin dissolves. In blender container, combine gelatin mixture, mayonnaise, vinegar, lime peel and juice and ice. Blend until ice is dissolved. Pour into mixing bowl. Add crabmeat with its juice and pickles; mix well and taste, adding salt and pepper if needed. Pour into 2-1/2 cup mold. Chill until firm, about 2 hours. To serve, quickly dip mold in a little warm water and un-mold onto lettuce-lined serving dish. Garnish with pimientos and radishes. Makes 1 large or 2 small servings.

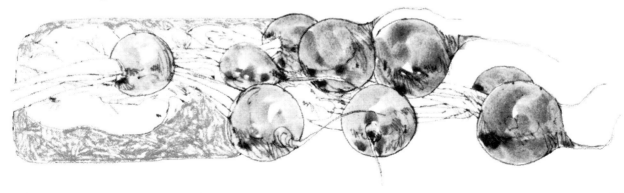

Calories: 358 or 179 per serving

CRAB MOUSSE

1/4 cup evaporated skim milk
1 can (6 ozs.) crabmeat, drained
    (save juice)
1/2 cup cold water
juice of one lemon
1 tsp. white vinegar

1 env. unflavored gelatin
1 env. instant onion broth or 1 tsp. onion powder
1 tbs. fresh chives
1/8 tsp. dried tarragon
salt and freshly ground pepper
2 tbs. imitation mayonnaise

Pour evaporated milk into small electric mixer bowl. Place beaters and bowl in freezer. Drain crabmeat and save juice. In saucepan, combine water, crab juice, lemon juice, vinegar, gelatin and seasonings. Place over low heat and stir until gelatin is dissolved. Refrigerate until gelatin begins to thicken. Remove evaporated milk from freezer. Whip milk using cold beaters, until stiff peaks form. Flake crabmeat with fork until very fine. Stir in mayonnaise. Fold gelatin mixture into whipped milk. Quickly fold in crabmeat. Pour mousse into individual mold. Refrigerate until firm. To serve, quickly dip mold into warm water and unmold onto lettuce-lined serving plate. Garnish with crisp green vegetables. Makes 1 large or 2 small servings.

Calories: 341 or 170 per serving

SHRIMP STUFFED TOMATOES

4 large firm ripe tomatoes, washed
1/2 tsp. salt
1/8 tsp. pepper
2 cups diced cooked shrimp
8 tbs. imitation mayonnaise
1/2-1 tsp. dried tarragon
1/4 tsp. each, thyme and curry powder
2 tbs. lemon juice

Core tomatoes and cut down from the top into quarters, cutting about two-thirds through the tomato. Gently open out tomatoes and sprinkle with salt and pepper. Combine remaining ingredients lightly and divide among the tomatoes, stuffing each with the mixture. Arrange tomatoes on lettuce-lined, chilled salad plates. Makes 4 servings.

Calories: 350 per serving

PINEAPPLE-COCONUT CHICKEN

An eye-filling salad like this also seems more stomach-filling.

1 medium fresh pineapple
1-1/2 cups (3 ozs.) uncooked very thin egg noodles,
    cooked in boiling salted water until barely tender, well drained
2 cups (8 ozs.) diced cooked chicken (1-1/2 lbs. uncooked chicken parts)
3 stalks celery, finely chopped
1 tsp. coconut flavoring (optional)
1/4 cup soy sauce
1/2 cup imitation mayonnaise
1 tsp. (or more) curry powder
ground ginger
1 medium banana, thinly sliced
1 orange or tangerine, separated into segments

Cut pinapple, including leaves, lengthwise in four sections. Cut out fruit, leaving only the leafy shells with about 1/2 inch of fruit lining. Drain shells upside down on paper

52

towels for at least a half hour. Chill shells and noodles. Cut pineapple meat in very small chunks, discarding fibrous center. Thoroughly drain in colander (reserve juice for snack). In mixing bowl, combine pineapple, chicken, celery and coconut flavoring. Chill. When ready to serve, drain off and discard juices from chicken mixture, toss with soy sauce and mayonnaise. Season with curry powder and ginger. Add banana. Fill each shell with a fourth of the noodles, cover with a fourth of the chicken mixture, decorate with citrus segments. Makes 4 servings.

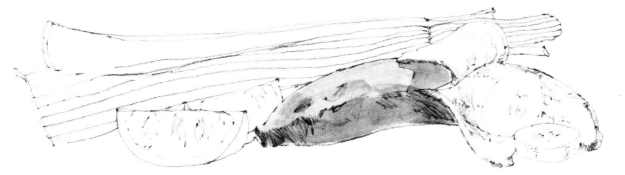

Calories: 330 per serving

CHICKEN SALAD

2 cups (8 ozs.) diced cooked chicken
1/3 cup (2 ozs.) diced bamboo shoots
1 cup fresh or drained canned bean sprouts
1 stalk celery, finely chopped
1/3 cup (2 ozs.) chopped green onions
1/4 cup each soy sauce and wine vinegar
1/4 tsp. ground ginger
2 cloves garlic, minced
Szechuan peppers, ground, or finely crushed red pepper
1 tsp. sugar or honey
1/4 cup imitation mayonnaise
lettuce leaves and parsley garnish

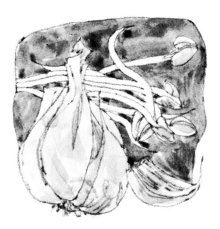

In bowl, combine first five ingredients. In saucepan, combine all other ingredients except mayonnaise, lettuce and parsley. Bring to boil and pour over salad; toss. Add mayonnaise and toss again. Chill. Serve on lettuce with parsley garnish. Makes 2 servings.

Calories: 350 per serving

HAM ROLLS

These cold, vegetable-stuffed rolls make a lovely hot weather luncheon plate. For color add a slice of melon.

1 cup (4 ozs.) cooked peas and carrots, drained
2 tbs. imitation mayonnaise
1 tbs. chopped chives or green onion tops
1 tbs. lemon or lime juice
salt, pepper and curry powder
4 slices (4 ozs.) lean Virginia or boiled ham
lettuce or romaine leaves
parsley sprigs or carrot curls for garnish

Mix vegetables, mayonnaise, chives and lemon juice thoroughly; season with salt, pepper and curry. Distribute evenly in center of each ham slice. Roll up. Arrange rolls on lettuce, garnish. Makes 2 servings.

Calories: 273 per serving

EGGS, CHEESE & VEGETABLES

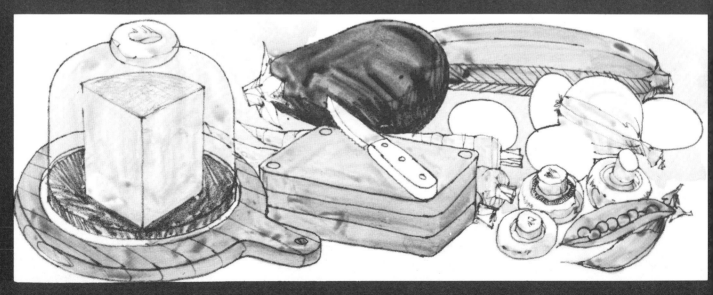

Too many calorie watchers have the wrong idea about eggs, cheese and vegetables. You can do more with eggs than just boil them. Cheese doesn't always mean an unadorned scoop of cottage cheese. And, vegetables aren't always boiled to death and bland.

The recipes I have created around these foods are among my most successful. You can even indulge in quiche and pizza without ruining your weight control program, because I have really s-t-r-e-t-c-h-e-d the calories in these recipes. Compare the calorie counts of my recipes to traditional quiche and pizza recipes.

Because the prices of meat will continue to climb, an investment in egg, cheese and vegetable recipes will not only save you money, but will be more healthy for your family too. When you see that a particular vegetable is in season, create a dinner around it—you'll really save money!

OMELETTE MOUSSEUSE

For a crunchy variation, stuff omelette with alfalfa sprouts.

2 large eggs, separated
1 tbs. minced chives
1 tsp. chicken seasoning (see page 6)
1/4 tsp. dried oregano
1/2 tsp. minced parsley
1/8 tsp. garlic powder

1/4 tsp. minced chervil (optional)
freshly ground pepper
pinch dill weed
    or 1/2 tsp. minced fresh dill
1 oz. extra sharp cheese, grated
2 tbs. butter or margarine

Combine egg yolks with herbs and chicken seasoning and beat with whisk until lighter in color. With rotary beater, beat egg whites until soft peaks form. Quickly beat yolk/herb mixture into egg whites. Preheat large non-stick skillet over medium heat. Pour in egg mixture, tilting pan for even distribution. Cover pan for about two minutes, checking underside of omelette with spatula once or twice. Sprinkle center with grated cheese. Cook only a few minutes longer. Center of omelette should be "baveuse," i.e., very moist and hardly cooked. Carefully flip one half of omelette towards center. Repeat with other half. Spread butter over folded omelette and let melt. Serve at once. Makes two luncheon servings.

Calories: 298 per serving

CARROT SOUFFLE

If you keep carrots, cheese and eggs in the refrigerator, you can whip up this meal-in-a-dish whenever time or energy are in short supply.

2 slices white bread
1 cup nonfat milk
1/4 small (1 oz.)onion
1 chicken bouillon cube
1/8 tsp. each nutmeg and thyme
8 small (12 ozs.)carrots, cooked

4 large eggs, separated
3/4 cup (3 ozs.) shredded sharp Cheddar cheese
1 tbs. minced parsley
freshly ground pepper
1/4 cup (1 oz.) grated Parmesan cheese
4 tsp. melted butter or margarine

In blender container combine bread, milk, onion, bouillon cube, nutmeg and thyme. Blend until smooth, pour into large saucepan. Cook over medium heat, stirring, until thickened. In blender container, combine carrots, egg yolks, Cheddar, parsley and pepper. Blend until smooth. Mix into sauce. Beat egg whites until stiff, but not dry. Fold carefully into carrot mixture. Pour into 4-6 cup souffle dish. Sprinkle with Parmeasan. Bake in 375^{0}F. oven for 30 minutes, or until center no longer jiggles when pressed. Divide butter over servings. Makes 4 servings.

Calories: 323 per serving

SPINACH SOUFFLE

Taste-testers agree: a delicious and easy main dish.

1 pkg. (10 ozs.) frozen chopped spinach, cooked
1 slice enriched white bread
1/2 cup nonfat milk
1 chicken bouillon cube
4 large eggs, separated
1-1/4 cups (4 ozs.) grated Parmesan or Romano cheese
1/2 tsp. onion powder
1/8 tsp. each garlic powder and nutmeg
freshly ground pepper
1 slice whole wheat bread, toasted and blended to fine crumbs
1 to 2 tsp. imitation bacon bits
4 tsp. melted butter or margarine

Drain spinach and squeeze dry. In blender container, combine white bread, milk and bouillon cube; blend until smooth, pour into small skillet. Cook over medium heat, stir-

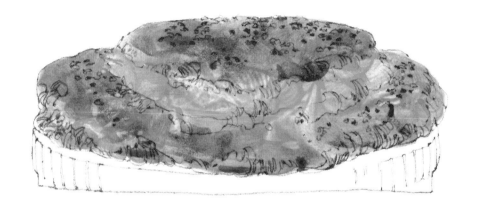

ring, until sauce thickens; return to blender. Add egg yolks, spinach, Parmesan, onion powder, garlic, nutmeg and pepper. Blend until smooth; pour into mixing bowl. Beat egg whites until stiff but not dry. Fold egg whites lightly, but evenly into sauce mixture. Pour into 4-6 cup souffle dish. Combine whole wheat crumbs and bacon bits; sprinkle on souffle with additional nutmeg if desired. Bake in 375°F. oven 20-25 minutes, or until center no longer jiggles when pressed. Divide butter over servings. Makes 4 servings.

Calories: 275 per serving

MUSHROOM SOUFFLE

The meaty flavor of mushrooms makes this light entree seem like a hearty meal.

2 cups (6 ozs.) sliced fresh mushrooms, or 2/3 cup sliced canned
2 slices white bread
1 cup nonfat milk
1/4 small (1 oz.) onion
1 chicken bouillon cube
1/4 tsp. garlic powder
freshly ground pepper
4 large eggs, separated
1/2 cup (2 ozs.) grated Parmesan cheese
nutmeg
4 tsp. melted butter or margarine

To cook fresh mushrooms: add 2 tablespoons water, 1/4 teaspoon salt and mushrooms to small nonstick saucepan. Cover, place over high heat and immediately reduce to low. Cook 5-7 minutes. Drain cooked or canned mushrooms and dry on paper towels. Chop very fine. In blender container combine bread torn into pieces, milk, onion, bouillon cube, garlic powder and pepper. Blend until smooth, pour into large saucepan. Cook over medium heat, stirring, until thickened. Cool to lukewarm. Blend in egg yolks gradually. Stir in mushrooms. Beat egg whites until stiff but not dry. Fold carefully into mushroom mixture. Pour into 4-6 cup souffle dish. Sprinkle with Parmesan and nutmeg. Bake at 375^{0}F. for 25 minutes, or until center no longer jiggles when pressed. Drizzle on butter. Makes 4 servings.

Calories: 228 per serving

63

CHEESE CREPES

You can enjoy melted cheese, a thick sauce studded with mushrooms, and a pancake, all without guilt.

1/2 cup (1-1/2 ozs.) sliced fresh mushrooms, or 3 tbs. sliced canned mushrooms
1/3 cup (1 oz.) shredded aged provolone cheese
2 tbs. imitation mayonnaise
1/8 tsp. garlic powder
salt and freshly ground pepper
1 slice white bread
1 large egg
1/4 cup buttermilk or yogurt
nutmeg

Cook fresh mushrooms, covered, in 1 tablespoon water just until limp. Drain fresh or canned mushrooms and chop very fine. In small bowl, combine mushrooms, cheese, mayonnaise, garlic powder, salt and pepper; reserve. In blender container, combine bread, egg, buttermilk and a pinch of nutmeg. Blend until smooth. Preheat nonstick skillet over medium heat. Pour in batter, tilting pan to spread evenly. Watch browning closely; check doneness by lifting edge with spatula. When brown-flecked or evenly browned, turn. Check carefully because crepe will tear if turned too soon. Brown other side. Spread all but 1-1/2 tablespoons filling over crepe. Cover skillet and cook over lowest heat just until cheese melts. Roll crepe and spread remaining filling over top. Cover and heat until cheese starts to melt. Makes 1 serving.

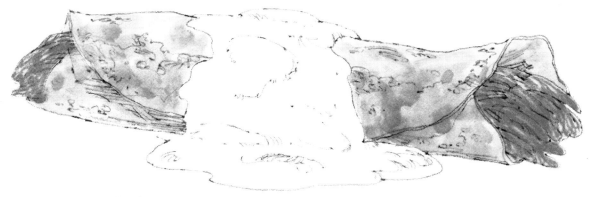

Calories: 398 per serving

CHEDDAR-ONION PIE

You'll enjoy preparing this often because it is easy and all of the ingredients are usually on hand.

4 medium (5 ozs. each) onions,
   very thinly sliced
2 tsp. chicken seasoning (see page 6)
freshly ground pepper
1/2 cup nonfat milk

2 cups (8 ozs.) shredded
   very sharp Cheddar cheese
1/3 cup instant nonfat dry milk
2 slices white bread, toasted
   and blended to fine crumbs
4 tsp. melted butter or margarine

Put onions in skillet and barely cover with water. Cook just until tender, but not soft. Drain well and arrange in 9-inch pie plate. Sprinkle with 1 teaspoon chicken seasoning and pepper. Slowly pour in milk. Sprinkle cheese on evenly. Combine dry milk, crumbs and remaining 1 teaspoon chicken seasoning; sprinkle on. Bake at 350^0F. for 25-30 minutes, or until nicely browned. Drizzle butter over top. Cool slightly before cutting. Makes 4 servings.

Calories: 320 per serving

CANNELLONI PIEDMONTESE

Cannelloni for a calorie-watcher? Is it possible? Si!

1-1/2 cups fresh spinach (washed, torn in small pieces and firmly packed)
1/3 cup (3 ozs.) ricotta or cottage cheese
1/2 tsp. onion powder
2 tsp. imitation bacon bits
garlic powder
salt and freshly ground pepper
1 slice whole wheat bread
1 large egg
1/4 cup nonfat milk or buttermilk
garlic powder and nutmeg
1 tsp. melted butter or margarine

Put spinach in small skillet without water, cover and steam over low heat just until wilted. Squeeze to remove moisture. Combine spinach, cheese, onion powder, bacon bits, a dash of garlic powder, 1/2 teaspoon salt and pepper. Blend by mashing with spoon. Set

68

aside. In blender container, combine bread torn in pieces, egg, milk, dash each of garlic powder and nutmeg. Blend until smooth, add salt and pepper to taste. Preheat large (8-10 inch) nonstick skillet over medium heat. Pour in batter, tilting pan to spread evenly. Watch browning closely; check doneness by lifting edge with spatula. When brown-flecked or evenly browned, turn. Check carefully because pancake will tear if turned too soon. Brown other side. Spread on spinach-cheese filling. Cover skillet and cook over lowest heat until cheese melts. Roll, put on serving plate, pour on butter. Makes 1 serving.

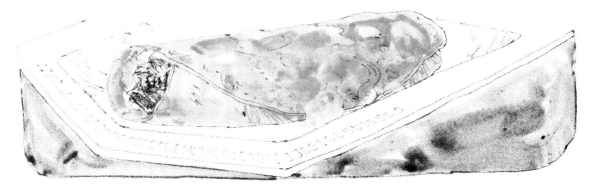

Calories: 326 per serving

QUICHE LORRAINE

Larousse Gastronomique, The Encyclopedia of Food, Wine and Cookery, says that the first quiches probably were made with crust of a bread paste, just as this one is.

4 slices whole wheat bread, toasted and blended into crumbs
1/3 cup instant nonfat dry milk
freshly ground pepper
2 cups nonfat milk
4 large eggs
1 tbs. minced parsley
4 tsp. imitation bacon bits
1 chicken bouillon cube
1/4 tsp. onion powder
salt
1-1/4 cups (4 ozs.) shredded aged or imported Swiss cheese
1/4 tsp. garlic powder
4 tsp. melted butter or margarine

70

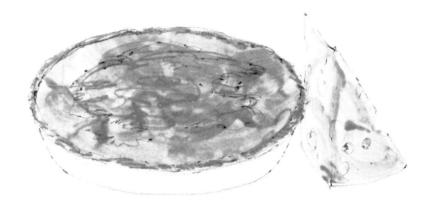

In 9-inch pie plate, combine crumbs, dry milk and pepper. Add just a few drops water to form a mixture that can be pressed into pan and up the sides for a crust. Chill half an hour. In blender jar, combine milk, eggs, parsley, bacon bits, bouillon cube and onion powder. Blend, add salt if needed. Pour slowly into crust. Sprinkle on cheese and garlic powder. Bake at 350°F. for 35 minutes, or until custard center no longer is liquid when pressed. Divide butter over servings. Makes 4 servings.

Calories: 330 per serving

CRAB AND CHEESE QUICHE

Even the French, who almost invented the calorie, now love their less-rich nouvelle cuisine, in which creative changes are encouraged.

chicken seasoning (see page 6)
1 medium (5 ozs.) onion, thinly sliced into rings
3 large eggs
2/3 cup (2 ozs.) shredded Swiss cheese
1/4 cup (1 oz.) grated Parmesan cheese
2 cups nonfat milk
1/4 tsp. garlic powder
salt and freshly ground pepper
4 ozs. crabmeat, drained and shredded (canned salmon is a delicious alternative)
4 tsp. imitation bacon bits
nutmeg or mace
4 tsp. melted butter or margarine

To a small nonstick skillet over medium-high heat, add just enough water to cover bot-

72

tom. Sprinkle on 1 teaspoon chicken seasoning and bring to boil. Quickly add onion and cook just until tender and lightly browned. Set aside. In blender container, combine eggs, Swiss cheese, Parmesan and 1 cup of the milk. Blend until smooth, pour into mixing bowl and stir in remaining milk, garlic powder and 1/2 teaspoon chicken seasoning. Taste and add salt and pepper. Fold in crabmeat. Pour into 9-inch pie plate. Sprinkle with bacon bits. Arrange onion on top. Sprinkle with nutmeg. Bake at 400^{0}F. for 10 minutes. Lower to 350^{0}F. and bake 25-30 minutes longer, or just until custard center is no longer liquid when pressed. Drizzle on butter. Makes 4 servings.

Calories: 260 per serving

PIZZA

Although we cannot de-calorize a thick-crusted pizzeria pizza topped with an inch of melted cheese and sausage, we can satisfy our craving for pizza with the following low-calorie version.

6 slices white bread, toasted and blended to medium-fine crumbs
2 cups instant nonfat dry milk
1-2 tbs. dried oregano leaves
salt and freshly ground pepper
2 cups (8 ozs.) shredded mozzarella
2 tbs. minced parsley
1/2 tsp. dried basil
3/4 cup tomato sauce
1/2 tsp. garlic powder
1-1/4 cup (4 ozs.) grated Parmesan
4 tbs. well-drained capers (optional)
2 tbs. olive oil

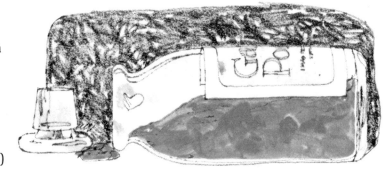

74

Combine crumbs, dry milk, oregano, salt, pepper and enough water to moisten mixture so that you can pat it out to line a 12-inch pizza pan sprayed with a no-stick vegetable spray. Fill with mozzarella, parsley, basil and more pepper. Carefully pour tomato sauce over filling. Sprinkle with garlic powder and Parmesan. Decorate with capers. Bake at 400°F. for 20-25 minutes or until crust is brown. Drizzle with oil. Lift around edges to prevent sticking; cool for 5 minutes before cutting. Makes 6 wedges.

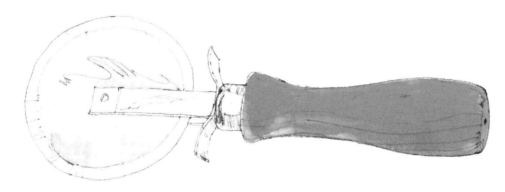

Calories: 396 per wedge

POTATO PANCAKES WITH APPLE SAUCE Germany

If you don't want to make apple sauce (recipe follows), buy the canned unsweetened type and jazz it up a bit with a dash of cinnamon and cloves. A half-cup is 50-60 calories.

1/3 cup finely shredded raw potato (4 oz. potato), drained
1/4 cup very finely minced green onion or 2 tbs. dried onion flakes
1 small egg, separated
1/3 cup instant nonfat dry milk
1 tsp. chicken seasoning (see page 6)
1 tsp. imitation bacon bits
nutmeg, freshly ground pepper and paprika
2 tsp. butter or margarine
Apple Sauce (instructions follow)

Cover potato with paper towels and press to dry thoroughly. Follow same procedure with fresh onions. In mixing bowl, combine potato, onions, egg yolk, dry milk, chicken seasoning, bacon and a pinch each of nutmeg, pepper and paprika. Beat egg white until stiff and very dry. Fold into potato mixture. Heat a nonstick skillet over low heat. Spoon on 5 pancakes, flatten each with spoon. Brown both sides very slowly or pancakes will have a raw taste. Sprinkle with more paprika. Top with butter, serve with apple sauce. Makes 1 serving.

APPLE SAUCE

1 medium cooking apple, peeled, cored, and sliced
1/2 cup water
1 env. sugar substitute
1 stick cinnamon, broken in half
1 whole clove

Into a small skillet over medium heat, put all sauce ingredients. Cover and simmer until apple is soft. Discard spices. Pour apples and juice into blender container. Blend until smooth. Cool.

Calories: 380 (including sauce)

MACARONI CHEESE BAKE

Macaroni, milk, eggs, two kinds of cheese and butter in a "diet" dish? Yes. One main-dish serving has fewer calories than a broiled steak.

1-1/4 cups (4 ozs.) uncooked elbow macaroni
2 cups nonfat milk
4 eggs
1 cup (3 ozs.) shredded Swiss cheese
1/4 tsp. garlic powder

salt and freshly ground pepper
1/4 cup (1 oz.) grated Parmesan or Romano
nutmeg
4 tsp. melted butter or margarine

Cook macaroni in boiling salted water; you should have 2-1/4 cups cooked; drain. Put macaroni in small baking dish. In blender container, combine milk, eggs, Swiss cheese and garlic powder. Blend until smooth. Taste and add salt and pepper. Pour over macaroni. Top with Parmesan and dust with nutmeg. Bake at 350°F. for 30-35 minutes, or until center feels nearly firm when touched. Drizzle on butter. Makes 4 servings.

Calories: 295 per serving

BROCCOLI AU GRATIN

U.S.A./Italy

1 slice whole wheat bread, toasted
    and blended to fine crumbs
1/3 cup (3 ozs.) ricotta or cottage cheese
1 large egg
1-1/2 tbs. lemon juice
1 cup nonfat milk
1 tbs. minced parsley

2 cloves garlic, minced
pinch nutmeg or mace
salt and freshly ground pepper
1 cup cooked broccoli spears, cut
    in 2-inch pieces
2 tsp. imitation bacon bits
2 tsp. melted butter or margarine

Make crumbs in blender jar, set aside. Wipe out jar and in it combine cheese, egg, lemon juice, milk, parsley, garlic and nutmeg. Blend until smooth. Season with salt and pepper. Put broccoli in 3-4 cup baking dish, mask with cheese mixture. Sprinkle with bacon bits. Bake at 350^{0}F. for 30-35 minutes, or until custard center is nearly set. Increase temperature to 400^{0}F. Sprinkle crumbs over top and bake until lightly browned. Drizzle with butter. Makes 1 full-meal or 2 luncheon servings.

Calories: 446 or 223 per serving

GINGER-GLAZED CARROTS

So many good low-calorie dishes have been inspired by Oriental cuisine.

1 lb. carrots
3 envs. sugar substitute
1 tsp. grated fresh ginger root or 1/4 tsp. ground ginger
1/4 cup soy sauce
1/4 tsp. garlic powder
2 tsp.-2 tbs. sesame oil (optional, see Introduction)

Cut carrots into strips of about the same size as slender French fries. In large frying pan combine carrots, sugar substitute, ginger and just enough water to cover. Simmer, covered, over medium heat until carrots are barely tender. Increase heat and cook uncovered until liquid has evaporated. Add soy sauce, garlic powder and oil. Toss and serve immediately. Makes 4 servings.

Calories: 103 per serving

SPINACH PIE

The unique flavor of Feta cheese brings ordinary spinach to life.

1 pkg. (10 ozs.) frozen chopped spinach
2/3 cup (4 ozs.) green onions, chopped
1 env. instant onion broth seasoning or 1 tsp. onion powder
2 large eggs, slightly beaten
2 ozs. Feta cheese, finely crumbled
1/2 cup skim evaporated milk
2 ozs. natural brown rice wafers or
      thin Norwegian flat bread
salt and freshly ground pepper
nutmeg
cinnamon
1 tbs. olive oil

Cook spinach according to package directions. Drain thoroughly and squeeze dry. Place in mixing bowl and set aside. In a non-stick skillet, using a very small amount of water

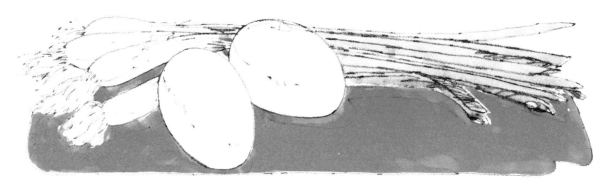

and some of the instant onion broth, quickly cook onions until tender. Drain and mix well with spinach. Stir in eggs and cheese. Add milk and stir until well mixed. Spread one-third of spinach mixture in medium-size baking dish. Make a second layer using one-third of crackers. Sprinkle with salt and pepper. Repeat layers until all spinach and crackers are used, ending with crackers. Dust last layer with nutmeg and cinnamon. Sprinkle top lightly with water to dampen. Bake in preheated 350°F. oven 20 to 25 minutes or until brown and slightly puffed. Drizzle olive oil evenly across top. Serve at once. Makes two servings.

Calories: 345 per serving

EGGPLANT PARMESAN

This recipe makes 2 light main-dish servings, but you can increase ingredients to make the number of servings you want. Non-dieters will never suspect that this is a lowered-calorie dish.

4 slices (3/4-inch thick) unpeeled eggplant
salt and freshly ground pepper
2 tbs. (1/2 oz.) grated mozzarella
2 tbs. (1/2 oz) grated Parmesan cheese
1/3 cup (3 ozs.) ricotta or cottage cheese
1/3 cup tomato sauce

2 tbs. buttermilk or yogurt
t tbs. minced parsley
1/4 tsp. each crumbled oregano
    and garlic powder
2 tsp. olive oil

Put eggplant in large skillet; add about 1 inch water. Simmer uncovered, turning, just until barely tender. Drain on paper towels, pat dry. Arrange side by side in baking dish. Sprinkle with salt and pepper and cover evenly with mozzarella, then Parmesan. Blend ricotta, tomato sauce, buttermilk, parsley, oregano and garlic powder. Spread over eggplant. Bake at 350^0F. for 25 minutes, or until eggplant is soft and top browned. Drizzle oil over slices. Makes 2 servings.

Calories: 190 per serving

STUFFED ZUCCHINI

2 medium (about 6 in. long) zucchini
2/3 cup cottage or ricotta cheese
1/4 to 1/2 tsp. garlic powder
   or 2 small garlic cloves, minced
2 tbs. chopped chives
2 tbs. chopped parsley

1/4 tsp. dried oregano
1/4 tsp. dried basil, crumbled
salt and freshly ground pepper
2 ozs. grated sharp cheese
1/2 cup tomato sauce
1 tbs. olive oil

Cut unpeeled zucchini in half lengthwise. Remove seeds and some of the meat to make hollow. Sprinkle with salt and turn onto paper towels for about 1/2 hour. Combine cheese and seasonings. Divide cheese mixture evenly and stuff each zucchini half. Arrange zucchini in overproof dish. Sprinkle each with grated cheese. Pour tomato sauce over cheese. Sprinkle with additional garlic and oregano. Add 1 inch water and bake, covered, in 350°F. oven about 30 minutes or until zucchini is tender. Uncover and increase oven temperature to 450°F. Bake until lightly browned. Just before serving drizzle each zucchini with olive oil. Makes two servings.

Calories: 267 per serving

SWEET STUFFED SQUASH

This can be either a main course or a vegetable dish.

1 large acorn or butternut squash, halved and seeded
2 large eggs
1 tsp. vanilla extract
2 tbs. brown sugar substitute
1/2 tsp. pumpkin pie spice
2/3 cup (6 ozs.) ricotta or cottage cheese
2 slices white bread, toasted and blended into crumbs

Place squash cut sides down in 9-inch square baking pan and add 2 tablespoons water. Cover with foil and bake at 350⁰F. about 40 minutes, or until pulp is tender. Scoop out squash, reserving shells. To blender container, add eggs, vanilla, squash, sugar, spice, cheese and part of the crumbs (save enough to sprinkle atop squash). Blend until smooth, adding a little water if necessary. Spoon into shells. Sprinkle with remaining crumbs. Bake uncovered at 450⁰F. for 10 minutes, or until puffed and hot. Makes 2 main-dish or 4 vegetable servings.

Calories: 275 or 136 per serving

RATATOUILLE NICOISE

France

The secret of good ratatouille is slow cooking, then letting the dish sit awhile, even refrigerated overnight. The secret of calorie watchers' ratatouille is omitting the enormous amount of olive oil traditionally used.

2 cups diced peeled eggplant
4 medium garlic cloves, minced
1/4 tsp. crumbled basil
2 green peppers, cut in strips
2 cups diced unpeeled zucchini

1/2 cup tomato sauce
salt and pepper
2 medium unpeeled tomatoes, diced
2 tbs. olive oil

In large frying pan, simmer eggplant in 2 tablespoons water with garlic and basil. When partially tender, add green pepper and cook until tender. Add zucchini, tomato sauce, salt and pepper. Cover and reduce heat to very low. Let barely simmer 15 minutes. Add diced tomato, cover and continue simmering until liquid is absorbed. Add salt if needed. Just before serving, sprinkle with oil and gently toss. Serve hot or at room temperature. Makes 4 servings.

Calories: 128 per serving

SEAFOOD

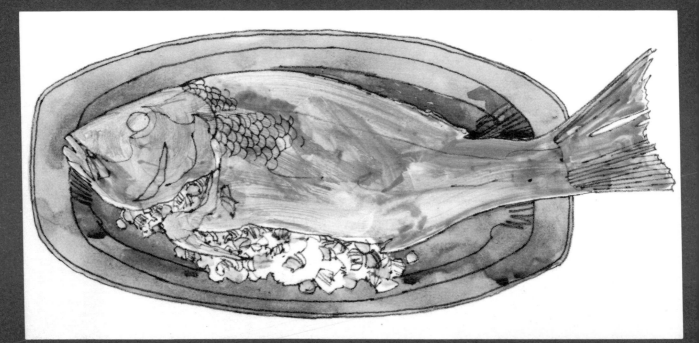

Because fish is low in calories and high in nutrition, it is considered a boon to a dieter. Many weight control programs advise eating fish up to five times a week. If you have not made your peace with preparing fish, you are missing an ally in the calorie department.

A fish is not JUST to fry. I hope you will try all of these recipes and expand your knowledge of cooking fish. But, for you traditionalists, here is a quick, simple way to have fried fish, calorie watcher's style: Mix 1/3 cup dry milk powder with 1 teaspoon onion powder. Dip fresh fillets of sole or flounder in mixture to coat both sides. Heat a non-stick skillet slowly and brown coated fish on both sides, about four minutes per side.

Here is the tartar sauce . . . our way: Mix 1 tablespoon plain yogurt, 1/4 cup fresh chopped chives, 1 tablespoon imitation mayonnaise, 1/4 teaspoon each salt and pepper, 1 teaspoon capers and fresh lemon juice, about 1 tablespoon. Serve over your cooked fillets.

SCALLOPS ST. JACQUES

A versatile dish—quick entree for 2 or appetizer for a very posh party if quantities are increased and the traditional white baking shells (coquilles) are used.

1 tbs. white vinegar
1 bay leaf
1 tsp. pickling spice
1/4 tsp. crumbled tarragon
8 ozs. uncooked scallops, halved
1/2 cup (2 ozs.) grated Parmesan cheese
2 large cloves garlic, pureed
4 tbs. imitation mayonnaise
1/4 cup buttermilk or yogurt
freshly ground pepper
2 slices white bread, toasted and blended to fine crumbs
1 lemon, half cut in wedges

In saucepan, bring 1 cup water, vinegar, bay leaf, spice and tarragon to a rolling boil.

Lower heat and add scallops. Simmer about 2 minutes, or just until scallops are no longer translucent inside. Remove scallops, drain (discard liquid) and arrange in 4 baking shells or 2 au gratin baking dishes. Combine Parmesan, garlic, mayonnaise, buttermilk and pepper. Pour over scallops. Top with crumbs and juice of half the lemon. Broil for 5 minutes, or until hot throughout and slightly brown. Serve with lemon wedges. Makes 2 servings.

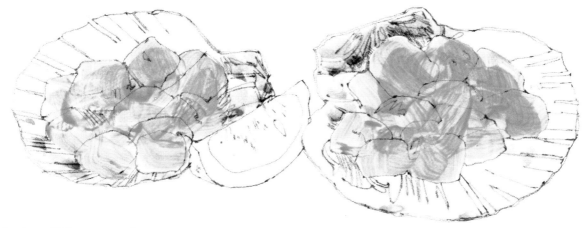

Calories: 370 per serving

OYSTERS AU GRATIN France

The French touch: Bake in large white shells or au gratin dishes.

1 cup nonfat milk
2 cloves garlic
2 slices white bread
1 tsp. chicken seasoning (see page 6)
1/4 tsp. onion powder
2 tbs. lemon juice
1/2 tsp. brandy flavoring (optional)
1 cup cooked or canned sliced mushrooms, drained
8 ozs. oysters, drained
salt, pepper and nutmeg
1/3 cup instant nonfat dry milk
1/4 tsp. crumbled tarragon

In blender container, combine milk and garlic; blend to puree garlic. Add bread in pieces, chicken seasoning and onion powder. Blend until smooth. Pour into medium skillet over medium heat and cook, stirring, until thickened. Stir in lemon juice, brandy flavoring, mushrooms and oysters. Mix thoroughly; add salt, pepper and 1/4 teaspoon nutmeg. Spoon into shells or au gratin baking dishes. Mix dry milk, tarragon, and a dash each of salt, pepper and nutmeg. Sprinkle over oyster mixture. Bake at 350^{0}F. for 15 minutes, or until top is brown and mixture bubbly. Makes 2 servings.

Note: To produce 1 cup cooked fresh mushrooms, start with 3 cups (9 ozs.) sliced mushrooms. Put mushrooms in nonstick pan, add 2 tablespoons water and 1/4 teaspoon salt; cover and place over high heat, immediately reduce to lowest heat and cook 10 minutes, or until softened.

SHRIMP CREOLE

Louisiana, U.S.A.

One secret of successful calorie watching is to top plain rice with a savory stew.

1/4 cup (2 ozs.) minced onion
2 stalks celery, chopped
1/2 cup tomato sauce
1/2 green pepper, chopped
1/2 cup sliced fresh mushrooms
    or 1/4 cup sliced canned mushrooms
1 bay leaf, crumbled
1/4 tsp. crumbled tarragon

1 tbs. minced parsley
1/2 tsp. dill weed
1/8 tsp. cayenne or liquid hot pepper sauce
1/2 cup clam juice
8 ozs. uncooked shrimp, peeled and deveined
juice of 1 lemon and salt
1 tsp. vegetable oil
rice, optional (see page 9)

In saucepan, combine onion, celery and tomato sauce. Simmer 5 minutes covered. Add green pepper, fresh mushrooms (add canned ones later), bay leaf, tarragon, parsley, dill weed, cayenne and clam juice. Cover and simmer about 15 minutes, or until mushrooms are tender. Add shrimp and canned mushrooms if used; cover and simmer about 5 minutes, just until shrimp are tender. Add lemon juice and salt. Drizzle oil over top. Makes 1 serving.

Calories: 270 per serving, 370 with rice

QUICK CURRIED SHRIMP

Indian-inspired

Make this in just 10 minutes. Serve with rice (see instructions for cooking the right amount for 1 person on page 9).

1 slice white bread, torn in pieces
1/2 cup evaporated or regular nonfat milk
1 tsp. chicken seasoning (see page 6)
1/2 tsp. curry powder, preferably the mild Madras type
1/8 tsp. each ground cardamom and garlic powder
pinch each black pepper, nutmeg and crushed red pepper
4 ozs. peeled cooked shrimp

In blender container, combine all ingredients except shrimp. Blend until smooth, adding more milk if too thick. Pour into saucepan. Simmer over medium heat, stirring, until thickened. Add shrimp just long enough to heat through. Makes 1 serving.

SHRIMP STUFFED WITH CRAB

Calorie watchers frequently have romantic dinners for two if they have watched their calories successfully. This elegant creation requires candlelight and an object of your affection.

12 ozs. jumbo uncooked unpeeled shrimp
2 slices white bread
1/2 cup nonfat milk
1/8 tsp. crumbled tarragon
1/8 tsp. garlic powder
4 ozs. drained crabmeat, saving 1 tbs. juice
juice of 1 lemon
salt and freshly ground pepper
pinch nutmeg and paprika
2 tbs. imitation mayonnaise

Peel and devein shrimp, leaving tails on. Cut each partially through lengthwise down the back to make pocket for stuffing. In blender container, combine bread torn in pieces, milk, tarragon and garlic powder. Blend until smooth. Pour into small skillet and simmer, stirring, until thickened. Remove from heat, add crab and lemon juice, mix well. Add salt and pepper as desired. Fill shrimp, patting mixture in firmly. Arrange side by side, filling side up, in the smallest possible baking dish. Sprinkle with nutmeg and paprika. Add 1 tablespoon each water and crabmeat juice to pan. Bake uncovered at 350⁰F. for 20-30 minutes, depending on size of shrimp, just until shrimp are tender. Top each with dab of mayonnaise to melt over filling. Makes 2 servings.

Calories: 370 per serving

SHRIMP TERIYAKI

A main dish for one or appetite-teaser for two.

8 ozs. large uncooked unpeeled shrimp
2 cloves garlic, minced
1/4 cup soy sauce
1/4 tsp. prepared mustard
1 tbs. tomato sauce

1 drop hot pepper sauce
1-1/2 envs. sugar substitute
2 tsp. wine vinegar
1/4 tsp. (or more) ground ginger
1 tbs. oil (Japanese use peanut oil)

Peel and devein shrimp, leaving tails on if you like. In saucepan, combine remaining ingredients except oil. Boil 1 minute, pour into bowl. Add shrimp, cover and marinate in refrigerator at least 2 hours, turning occasionally. Thread shrimp on skewers (soak wooden ones in water to prevent burning). Broil 6 inches below heat approximately 5 minutes on each side, basting often with marinade and oil. Makes 1 main-dish serving or 2 appetizers.

Calories: 390 or 195 per serving

COD CROQUETTES

2 slices whole wheat bread
about 2 cups (8 ozs.) flaked cooked cod or other fish
1 cup minced cooked or canned mushrooms, drained
2 tbs. each minced parsley and chives
4 (or less) cloves garlic, minced
2 tbs. imitation mayonnaise
salt and freshly ground pepper
1/3 cup instant nonfat dry milk
1 tsp. onion powder

Toast bread, dry and blend into fine crumbs. With fork, finely crumble fish. Add crumbs, mushrooms, parsley, chives, garlic, mayonnaise, salt and pepper. Mix thoroughly and, adding water if necessary, form into 4 patties. Mix dry milk with onion powder. Roll patties in mixture. In preheated nonstick skillet over medium-low heat, slowly brown patties, turning often. Makes 2 servings.

Calories: 243 per serving

CALDERATA

It's a full meal made in one pan and customarily served by Portuguese fishermen in a soup bowl.

2 medium tomatoes, very thinly sliced
1 small (3-4 ozs.) potato, very thinly sliced
6 ozs. fillet of cod, cut in chunks
1 medium onion (5 ozs.), very thinly sliced
4 cloves garlic, minced
salt and freshly ground pepper
crushed red pepper
1/4 cup tomato sauce
2 tsp. olive oil

In skillet make layers of half the tomato slices, then half the potatoes, half the fish and half the onion, seasoning as you go with garlic, salt, black pepper and red pepper. Repeat similar layers of each ingredient with seasoning. Pour on tomato sauce. Cover and simmer over low heat 20 minutes, or until vegetables are tender. Drizzle with oil. Makes 1 serving.

Calories: 445 per serving

SOLE WITH GRAPE SAUCE

Greece

In this Greek creation chopped grapes are blended into a spinach sauce, lending tang and sweetness. The recipe serves two—you and another adventuresome sort. However, increasing quantities to party proportions is easy.

8 ozs. fillet of sole
1/2 cup cooked spinach, drained
3/4 cup (3 ozs.) chopped green onions
1 tbs. chopped parsley
1/2 tsp. dill weed
1/2 tsp. crumbled oregano
salt and freshly ground pepper

1 slice white bread
1/2 cup nonfat milk
dash nutmeg
1 cup firm seedless green grapes
2 tbs. water
lemon juice (about 1 lemon)
1 tbs. melted butter or margarine

Rinse fish and pat dry with paper towels. Squeeze spinach dry. Boil onions in a small amount of water for 1 minute. Drain well. Combine spinach, onions, parsley, dill weed, oregano, salt and pepper. Spread filling on each fish fillet. Roll fillets and secure with picks. Arrange side by side in the smallest baking dish possible. In blender container combine bread torn in pieces, milk and nutmeg. Blend until smooth. Pour into small skillet over medium heat and simmer, stirring, until thickened. Remove from heat and set aside. Coarsely chop grapes; add with juices to small saucepan; add as little water as possible to prevent burning as you simmer grapes for 5 minutes, or just until softened but no liquid remains. Stir grapes into sauce, pour over fish. Cover and bake at 350^{0}F. for 15-20 minutes, or until fish is no longer translucent inside. Add lemon juice to taste to pan juices. Drizzle butter on servings. Makes 2 servings.

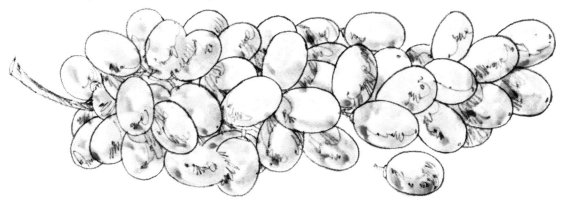

Calories: 259 per serving

FILLET OF SOLE NORMANDY

Elegant and delectable—fish rolled around shrimp, topped with two sauces and rimmed with mushrooms.

8 ozs. medium uncooked shrimp, peeled and deveined
8 ozs. fillet of sole
1 cup sliced fresh mushrooms, or 1/2 cup whole canned button mushrooms
salt and pepper
juice of 1 lemon
bouquet garni of 1 bay leaf, 3 whole black peppers and 1/4 tsp. dried tarragon
1 slice white bread
1/2 cup nonfat milk
1 tsp. chicken seasoning (see page 6)
1/4 tsp. onion powder
nutmeg
1 tbs. tomato sauce mixed with 1 tbs. butter or margarine, warmed

Roll shrimp inside fish this way: cut fish into as many pieces as there are shrimp, making sure each is large enough to wrap around a shrimp. Roll each tightly around a shrimp, secure with picks. Simmer fresh mushrooms with 1 tablespoon water, 1/8 teaspoon salt and a dash pepper just until soft, about 5 minutes (merely heat and season canned mushrooms); cover and keep warm. To a large skillet, add 1/2 inch water, 1 tablespoon of the lemon juice and bouquet garni. Bring to boil, reduce heat to lowest and add rolls. Poach uncovered in barely simmering water about 10 minutes, or just until fish is no longer translucent inside. Meanwhile make the main sauce: in blender container, combine bread torn in pieces, milk, chicken seasoning and onion powder; blend until smooth. Pour into small skillet over medium heat and cook, stirring until thickened. Mix in remaining lemon juice, salt, pepper and pinch of nutmeg. Arrange fish rolls on serving platter, pour on sauce. Drain mushrooms, pat dry and pour around edge. Dot rolls with tomato-butter sauce. Makes 2 servings.

Calories: 325 per serving

SPINACH RING WITH SALMON

Spinach custard baked in a ring mold filled with salmon and mushrooms, a real showpiece meal for two.

1 pkg. (10 ozs.) frozen chopped spinach
2 slices whole wheat bread
1 tsp. chicken seasoning (see page 6)
1 tsp. onion powder
dash nutmeg
1 cup nonfat milk
1/2 tsp. brandy extract (optional)
2 large eggs, beaten
1 cup sliced fresh mushrooms, or 1/3 cup sliced canned mushrooms
4 ozs. canned salmon, drained and flaked
2 tbs. imitation mayonnaise
2 tsp. fresh lemon juice
salt and freshly ground pepper

Cook spinach, drain and squeeze dry. In blender container, combine bread torn in pieces, chicken seasoning, onion, nutmeg and milk; blend until smooth. Pour into small skillet over medium heat and cook, stirring, until thickened; remove from heat. Add brandy flavoring, spinach and eggs. Mix well. Pour into 3-cup ring mold. Set mold in baking pan, add 1 inch hot water to pan. Bake at 350°F. for 30 minutes, or until center no longer is liquid when pressed. Meanwhile, if mushrooms are fresh, cook with 1/8 teaspoon salt and 1 tablespoon water, covered, just until soft. To serve hot: heat mushrooms in their liquid, drain; add salmon, mayonnaise, lemon juice, salt and pepper; mix, heating gently, until all is warm. Unmold hot spinach ring onto serving plate, fill with warm salmon mixture. To serve cold: fill unmolded spinach ring with unheated salmon mixture; chill. Makes 2 servings.

BAKED STUFFED FISH

On the East Coast I use a very small bluefish. On the West Coast you may find whole cod, perch and rockfish of the proper size. Inland cooks may want to try trout, catfish or lake bass.

1 whole (about 1-1/4 lbs.) fish, cleaned, with head and tail removed if you prefer
1/4 tsp. ground thyme
salt and freshly ground pepper
1 stalk celery, finely chopped
1/2 cup (2 ozs.) thinly sliced carrot
1/2 medium onion (2 ozs.), sliced into thin rings
1 lemon (including peel), sliced into thin rings
2 or 3 garlic cloves, minced
1 tbs. crumbled oregano
2 tsp. olive oil

Heat oven to 350⁰F. Wash inside of fish and dry with paper towels. Dust inside with thyme, salt and pepper. Combine celery, carrots, onion, lemon, garlic and oregano. Stuff fish with half of mixture, lay in baking dish. Cover with remaining mixture. Sprinkle with salt and pepper. Cover dish with foil. Bake 20-25 minutes, or until fish no longer is translucent inside. (Add a little water if needed during baking.) Drizzle oil over fish and leave in oven 1 minute longer for oil to be absorbed. Serve hot. Makes 1 serving.

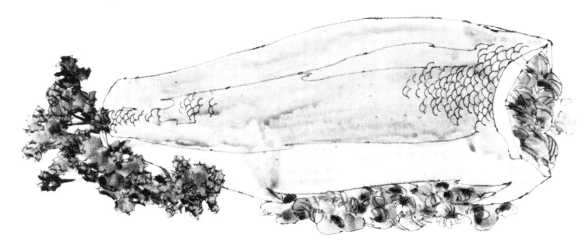

Calories: 300 per serving

CURRIED TUNABURGERS

This is a jiffy dish for people on the go. Serve topped with mustard and a garnish of crisp fresh vegetables.

1 slice whole wheat bread
4 ozs. well-drained tuna
1 tbs. minced onion
1/2 tsp. curry powder
1/4 tsp. each dill weed, garlic powder and cumin
salt and freshly ground pepper
1/4 tsp. prepared mustard
1 tbs. minced parsley
nonfat milk

Toast bread until dry. Blend into medium-fine crumbs. Combine all ingredients, using just enough milk to moisten mixture so it can be shaped into 2 thin, firm patties. Broil about 6 minutes on each side, or until brown and crisp. Makes 1 serving.

Calories: 278 per serving

TUNA QUADRATTINI

1 cup cooked spinach
salt and freshly ground pepper
1 cup fresh mushroom slices
6 ozs. water-packed tuna, drained
1 clove garlic, minced
1 bay leaf

1/4 tsp. crumbled dried basil
1/2 tsp. Tabasco sauce
1/2 cup tomato sauce
1 cup cooked noodles
1/3 cup (1 oz.) grated Romano cheese
nutmeg

Drain spinach and squeeze dry. Season with salt and pepper. Spread mushroom slices out in shallow pan. Broil until crisp. Reserve mushroom juice. In mixing bowl, combine tuna, mushrooms and their juice, garlic, bay leaf, basil, Tabasco and 1/4 cup of the tomato sauce. Mix well. Pour remaining tomato sauce into small baking dish. Add a layer of noodles, a layer of spinach and a layer of tuna mixture until all are used. Sprinkle top with Romano and a little nutmeg. Bake in 350°F. oven about 35 minutes or until top is brown. Serve at once. Makes 2 servings.

CHICKEN

Chicken is not only permitted, but usually encouraged on almost all diets. It is low in calories and the ways it can be prepared are almost endless.

When you are counting calories, the skin must be removed either prior to cooking or just after. I prefer to discard it before cooking. The lovely flavor the skin develops while it is cooking is just too much for me to resist. I live happier (and thinner) without temptation.

I use arrowroot or bread instead of flour and butter as thickening agents in these sauces. This will save you many calories. Fruit sweetens and delicately flavors some dishes which will delight your palate.

The chicken should be the official bird of calorie watchers.

CHICKEN WITH ORANGE SAUCE

Tangy satisfaction for your sweet tooth.

8 ozs. uncooked chicken pieces, skin removed
1 tsp. chicken seasoning (see page 6)
1/4 tsp. onion powder
1 slice white bread
1/4 tsp. grated fresh orange peel
1/2 cup orange juice

2 envs. sugar substitute
1/8 tsp. each cinnamon and garlic powder
1/4 tsp. prepared mustard
1/2 tsp. orange extract
salt and freshly ground pepper
1 tbs. butter or margarine

Dust chicken with chicken seasoning and onion powder. Arrange on aluminum foil in broiler pan. Broil 6 inches from heat until tender and no longer pink inside, about 10-12 minutes per side. Meanwhile make sauce: in blender container, combine bread torn in pieces, orange peel, orange juice, sugar substitute, cinnamon, garlic powder, mustard and extract. Blend until creamy. Pour into skillet over medium heat and cook, stirring constantly, until thickened. Add salt and pepper. Serve chicken with sauce poured on top, dotted with butter. Makes 2 servings.

Calories: 300 per serving

CHICKEN DETENTE

The classic Chicken Kiev, oozing with butter, has been "de-calorized" into this version, a peaceful solution to outright war against overweight.

5 ozs. sliced chicken boneless breast halves
MSG (monosodium glutamate)
2 tsp. chicken seasoning (see page 6)
1/4 tsp. onion powder

3 tbs. chopped fresh chives
3 tbs. nonfat dry milk
1 tbs. melted butter or margarine

Using a meat mallet, pound each chicken piece paper thin. Dust both sides delicately with MSG. Dust one side of each piece with a total of 1 teaspoon chicken seasoning and the onion powder; sprinkle with chives. Roll each (seasoning inside) lengthwise in a long, tight roll; fasten with wooden picks. Mix dry milk with remaining 1 teaspoon chicken seasoning. Roll chicken in mixture. Choose small baking dish just large enough to hold rolls side by side; line with foil. Add rolls and 1/4 inch water. Cover rolls loosely with foil. Bake at 350°F. for 15-20 minutes, or just until brown and tender. Don't overcook. Drizzle with butter. Makes 1 serving.

Calories: 275 per serving

SPICY CHICKEN

Although this family entree is a great favorite with children, the calorie count is low enough for plump parents.

1 uncooked chicken, cut into pieces
about 1 tbs. curry powder, preferably the mild Madras type
garlic powder
ground ginger
salt

Set oven at 350^0F. Remove and discard chicken skin. Line baking pan with foil; on it arrange chicken pieces side by side. Sprinkle each lavishly with curry, then garlic powder. Now, more delicately, sprinkle on ginger, then just a little salt. Bake uncovered about 30 minutes. Turn pieces and season again the same way. Bake about 30 minutes more, or until a crisp, brown crust has formed.

Calories: about 150 per 6 oz. serving

SWEET-SOUR GINGERED CHICKEN

Oriental people, who are hardly ever overweight, seldom eat desserts. Could this be because they satisfy their sweet tooths sooner with just a little sugar in many main dishes like this?

8 ozs. uncooked chicken pieces, skin removed
2 stalks celery, cut in chunks
1/4 cup soy sauce
2-1/2 tbs. white vinegar
1-1/2 envs. sugar substitute

1/2 tsp. ground or grated ginger root
1 tsp. grated fresh orange peel
2/3 cup dietetic pineapple carbonated
  beverage or orange soda
1 tbs. dried onion flakes

Marinate chicken in all ingredients at least 2 hours or overnight in the refrigerator. Remove celery and put it in small skillet, barely cover with water and simmer uncovered until tender and liquid is absorbed. Remove chicken from marinade and place in small baking dish. Into blender container, pour marinade and celery; blend until smooth. Mask chicken with sauce. Cover with foil and bake at 350°F. for 45-50 minutes. Remove foil and bake about 20 minutes, or until chicken is tender. Makes 1 serving.

CROQUETTES DE VOLAILLE

2 cups (6 ozs.) thinly sliced fresh mushrooms
salt, pepper and thyme
3/4 cup (4 ozs.) minced cooked chicken
1 egg, beaten
1 slice white bread, toasted and blended into crumbs
1 tsp. minced parsley
1 tsp. chicken seasoning (see page 6)
1/4 tsp. onion powder
instant nonfat dry milk
1 egg, separated
1 slice white bread
1/2 cup nonfat milk
pinch nutmeg
2 tsp. lemon juice
1 tbs. butter or margarine

First prepare mushrooms to serve around croquettes: into small saucepan, put mushrooms, 2 tablespoons water, 1/4 teaspoon salt and a dash each pepper and thyme. Cover and place over high heat, immediately reduce to lowest heat and cook 5-10 minutes (reheat and drain before serving). To make croquettes: mix chicken, the beaten egg, half the crumbs, parsley, chicken seasoning and onion powder. Form several oval croquettes. (If mixture is too moist, add dry milk powder to firm.) Beat egg white, roll croquettes in it, then in remaining crumbs. Bake at 400°F. until golden brown, about 10 minutes. Meanwhile make sauce: to blender jar, add remaining bread slice torn in pieces, liquid milk and nutmeg. Blend until smooth. Pour into small skillet over low heat and stir constantly just until it boils; remove from heat. Add lemon juice, butter, salt and pepper. Cover to keep warm. Just before serving, beat egg yolk and stir into sauce. Return to very low heat, stirring constantly, just until thickened. (Don't let simmer or egg will curdle.) Pour sauce over croquettes and place mushrooms around edge. If desired, dust lightly with nutmeg. Makes 2 servings.

CHICKEN POLENTA

This svelte version of North Italy's polenta should appeal to Americans, especially those from the corn-growing and corn-eating regions. Green beans, including the Italian variety available frozen, make an excellent side dish.

5 ozs. uncooked chicken, skin removed
1 tsp. chicken seasoning (see page 6)
3/4 cup tomato sauce
1/4 cup water
2 cloves garlic, minced
salt and freshly ground pepper
1/2 tsp. crumbled basil
a few rosemary leaves, crumbled
1 medium green pepper, cut in strips
1/3 cup (3 ozs.) chopped onion

Polenta:
1 cup water
1/4 tsp. salt
dash of cayenne or plenty of black pepper
1 beef bouillon cube
3 tbs. (1 oz.) yellow cornmeal

In nonstick frying pan, brown chicken by sprinkling with chicken seasoning and just enough water to coat; turn in pan juice to coat, adding more water if necessary. Then add all other ingredients except those for polenta and simmer for 40 minutes, or until chicken is tender, adding salt and pepper if desired. Cover and keep warm. Meanwhile, make polenta: To saucepan, add the 1 cup water, 1/4 teaspoon salt, cayenne and bouillon cube; bring to a rolling boil. Gradually sprinkle cornmeal over water, stirring constantly, just until a thick mush forms. Remove from heat, cover and let sit for 5 minutes before serving. Top with chicken. Makes 1 serving.

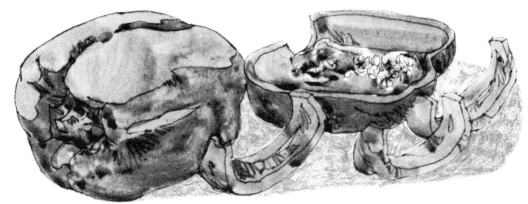

CHICKEN CACCIATORA

The filling and aromatic old favorite made less fattening.

5 ozs. chicken pieces, skin removed
2 tsp. chicken seasoning (see page 6)
1 cup tomato juice
1/4 tsp. crumbled basil
1 bay leaf
1/2 medium green pepper, cut in strips

1 cup (3 ozs.) thinly sliced fresh mushrooms,
    or 1/3 cup sliced canned mushrooms
2 cloves garlic, minced
2 tbs. (1 oz.) minced onion
salt and freshly ground pepper
2 tsp. olive or salad oil

In a nonstick skillet over medium-high heat, brown chicken by adding a tablespoon or two of water and the chicken seasoning; brown by turning in the pan juice, adding more water if necessary. Add all other ingredients except oil and, if used, the canned mushrooms should be added 15 minutes later. Cover and simmer about 30 minutes, or until chicken is tender. Drizzle oil over the top. Makes 1 serving.

Calories: 320 per serving

CHICKEN A LA KING IN TOAST CUPS

The Belgian "a la king," Bouchees a la Reine, different from the American dish of the same name, tastes royally rich enough to be deposited in a Swiss bank account.

1 slice whole wheat bread
1 cup (3 ozs.) sliced fresh mushrooms
2 tbs. (1 oz.) minced onion
salt and freshly ground pepper
1/2 cup nonfat milk
1 slice white bread
pinch nutmeg
1/4 tsp. garlic powder
1/2 cup (2 ozs.) diced cooked chicken
1 hard-cooked egg, chopped
1/2 tsp. lemon juice
2 tsp. melted butter or margarine

To make toast cups: With serrated knife, carefully cut whole wheat bread in half through crust to make 2 very thin slices. (A very slight toasting will make slicing easier.) Slightly dampen bread with a few drops of water to soften, then roll paper thin with rolling pin. Mold each slice into a custard cup or muffin tin to form a cup shape. Reserve to bake just before serving time. To make chicken filling: to small nonstick saucepan, add fresh mushrooms, onion, 1/8 teaspoon salt, pepper and 1 tablespoon water. Cover, place over high heat, immediately turn heat to lowest possible and cook 10 minutes. (If canned mushrooms are used, just simmer with onion and no salt for 5 minutes.) Drain mushrooms, reserve. In blender container, combine milk, white bread torn in pieces, nutmeg and garlic powder. Blend until smooth. Pour into small skillet over medium heat, stir constantly just until it boils. Add chicken, egg, mushroom mixture, lemon juice, salt and pepper to taste. Remove from heat and keep warm. Bake toast cups at 350^{0}F. until golden brown, about 10 minutes. Fill, drizzle butter over tops. Makes 1 full-meal serving or 2 small servings.

Calories: 409 or 205 per serving

WATERZOOI KIEKEN

Brown rice is my favorite accompaniment for this homey chicken stew.

2 lbs. chicken parts, skin removed
8 stalks celery, minced
3-4 (8 ozs.) leeks (white part only), chopped
1-2 cups coarsely chopped green onions (including tops)
2 chicken bouillon cubes
1/4 cup minced parsley
bouquet garni of 2 crushed bay leaves, 10 whole black peppers
    and 5 whole cloves tied in cheesecloth
1 tsp. dill weed
1 tsp. each ground sage and thyme
salt and freshly ground pepper
1/4 cup butter or margarine
1/2 cup evaporated or regular nonfat milk
1 tbs. wine or brandy flavoring (optional)

126

Put chicken in large saucepan and surround with celery, leeks, onion, and bouillon cubes. Add water to about halfway point. Add herbs, salt and pepper. Bring to a boil, cover, lower heat and simmer for 45 minutes, or until chicken is tender. (Check water frequently so that you will finish with a greatly reduced broth.) Just before serving, stir in butter, milk, flavoring, more salt and pepper if needed. Makes 4 servings.

Note: If you can't find leeks, leave them out or substitute 1 large mild white onion. If you don't want to make a bouquet garni, use 2 whole bay leaves, extra ground black pepper and several dashes ground cloves instead.

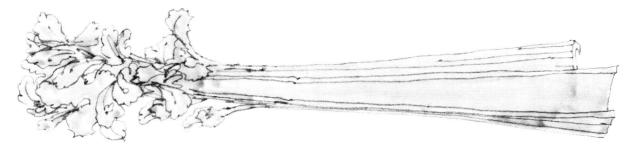

Calories: 270 per serving

MEATS

For many of us, a meal isn't a meal without meat. It sets the tone, and we plan all the other dishes around it.

Meat is high in protein, unfortunately, it can also be high in calories. Proper handling and moderation is the key. Pork, often forbidden on diets, can be enjoyed by a calorie watcher, if much of the fat is eliminated. This is not difficult to accomplish.

If you have not tried ground lamb before, you might be pleased with the discovery. The Greeks have a particular knack for creating delicious meals with lamb. I have included many adaptations from their recipes that you can enjoy. Don't be surprised if the hamburger fanatic in your family becomes a fan of Moussaka or Stuffed Cabbage Rolls.

Meat doesn't have to be boring and bland for calorie watchers. Try some of the following delicious recipes.

BARBECUED BEEF RIBS

Buy long beef ribs, not those that have been cut into short lengths. Meat markets can save these ribs for you. They are what is left after a butcher trims the rib section to make boneless rib steaks or rolled rib roasts. Unlike pork spareribs, beef ribs are not very fatty and the meat is tender enough to broil.

12 beef ribs
6 cloves garlic, pureed
3/4 cup soy sauce
1/2 tsp. ground ginger
1/2 cup wine vinegar
10 whole black peppers
2 bay leaves
1/4 cup brown sugar substitute
2/3 cup instant nonfat dry milk
1 cup unsweetened crushed pineapple, drained

In flat dish, lay ribs side by side. In skillet, combine rest of the ingredients except milk

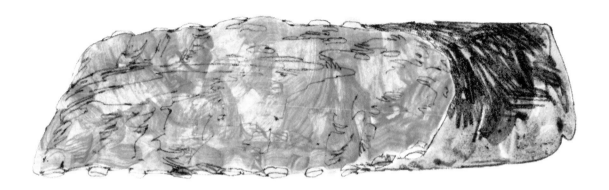

powder and pineapple; bring to a boil and pour warm over ribs. Cover and refrigerate several hours or overnight, turning occasionally. Drain and reserve marinade. Coat one side of ribs with half the milk powder; arrange milk-side up on rack in broiler pan. Broil 6 inches below heat for 12-15 minutes, basting occasionally with marinade. Turn ribs, coat other side with remaining milk powder. Broil 10 minutes and spread pineapple evenly over the top. Return to broiler just until fruit browns and forms a bubbly glaze that sticks to the ribs. Cook just until meat is medium rare or it will toughen. Makes 6 servings.

Calories: 353 per serving

SWEET-SOUR MEATBALLS

Hawaii

Accompany with a half cup of hot wide egg noodles or rice (per serving) to compliment the Oriental seasonings.

1/2 cup unsweetened crushed pineapple, drained (save juice)
1 stalk celery, minced
2 tbs. soy sauce
1 tsp. vinegar
1/4 tsp. ground ginger or 1 tsp. grated fresh ginger
1 envs. sugar substitute
8 ozs. ground beef chuck
1/4 tsp. each onion powder and garlic powder
1/3 cup instant nonfat dry milk
salt and freshly ground pepper
1/2 green pepper, cut in 3/4-inch pieces

To saucepan, add several tablespoons pineapple juice and celery; simmer celery, adding juice as necessary, just until tender. Drain if necessary and add soy sauce, vinegar, ginger, sugar substitute and pineapple. Simmer several minutes, or until some of the liquid has evaporated; cover and remove from heat; reserve. In bowl, combine beef, onion powder, garlic powder, milk powder, salt and pepper. Mix well and form into small meatballs, adding a little water if necessary. Balls should be firm, but moist. Using short skewers, spear meatballs with pieces of green pepper in between. If wooden skewers are used, soak in water first to prevent burning. Arrange skewers on rack in broiler pan and broil 6 inches below heat for 5-6 minutes on each side, or until meat is no longer pink inside. Meanwhile, reheat sauce. Serve meatballs on skewers with sauce poured on top. Makes 2 servings.

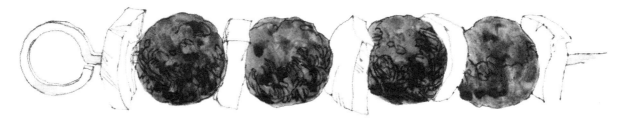

Calories: 339 per serving

PASTITSO

Americans who like macaroni casseroles naturally take to this Greek version.

1/3 cup (1-1/2 ozs.) uncooked orzo or small macaroni
8 ozs. ground beef chuck
1/3 cup (2 ozs.) finely chopped onion
2 cloves garlic, minced
2/3 cup tomato sauce
1 tbs. chopped parsley or 1 tsp. dried parsley
1/4 tsp. sherry flavoring (optional)
1/4 tsp. cinnamon
salt and freshly ground pepper
1/3 cup nonfat milk
nutmeg
3 tbs. instant nonfat dry milk

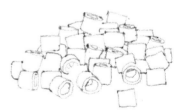

Cook macaroni in boiling salted water; drain and measure 1 heaping tablespoon into blender container. Line a 4-cup size baking dish with half the remaining macaroni; reserve

the rest. Mix beef and onion; form into thin patty and put on rack in broiler pan. Broil until fat has dripped out but meat is still moist. Immediately crumble with fork and mix with garlic, tomato sauce, parsley, sherry flavoring, cinnamon, salt and pepper. Spread meat evenly across macaroni in baking pan; cover with reserved macaroni. Make sauce: to the 1 tablespoon macaroni in blender container, add the liquid milk and dash of nutmeg. Blend until smooth and pour into small skillet over medium-high heat. Cook, stirring, until thickened. Remove from heat and stir in milk powder. Spread evenly on macaroni in baking pan; sprinkle delicately with cinnamon and nutmeg. Bake uncovered at 350^{0}F. for 25-30 minutes, or until crusty on top. Makes 2 servings.

Calories: 356 per serving

GRINGO ENCHILADAS

This recipe is one of my favorites. The enchiladas may not be authentic (made with tortillas), but they can be prepared with foods from any Americano grocery store.

1 lb. ground beef chuck
1/2 tsp. onion powder
1-2 tbs. chili powder
4 cloves garlic, minced
1/4 cup tomato sauce
1/8 tsp. ground cumin (optional)
salt and freshly ground pepper
1 cup canned kidney beans, drained
4 slices whole wheat bread
2 tsp. olive or other salad oil

Mix beef with onion powder. Form 2 thin patties and put on rack in broiler pan. Broil on each side until fat has dripped out but meat is still moist. Immediately crumble with fork; add 1-2 tablespoon chili powder, garlic, tomato sauce, cumin, salt and pepper; mix.

136

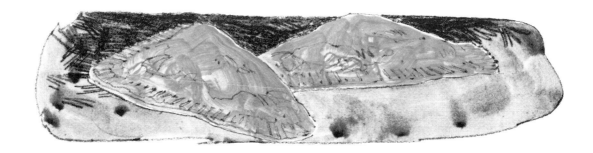

Meanwhile, in blender jar, puree beans until smooth. Add to meat mixture and adjust seasonings; reserve for filling. Make "tortilla" wrappers from the bread this way: Sprinkle bread very lightly on both sides with chili powder. With rolling pin, roll each slice as thin as possible without tearing. Spoon an equal amount of the filling onto the center of each slice. Fold bread over to form triangle-shaped turnover; seal edges by moistening with water and pressing with tines of a fork. Lift with spatula onto baking sheet. Bake uncovered at 350°F. for 15 minutes, or until toasted and hot. Drizzle with oil, serve at once. Makes 4 servings.

Calories: 362 per serving   **137**

TAMALE PIE

Americans have used tamale flavors to create a popular casserole, Tamale Pie. Here I have adapted the old favorite for calorie watchers. My pie is a "cobbler," with cornmeal crust on top instead of the bottom. This is a sure winner at a potluck or buffet dinner.

8 ozs. ground beef chuck
1/2 tsp. onion powder
2/3 cup tomato sauce
1-2 tbs. chili powder
2 cloves garlic, minced
salt
1/2 small (2 ozs.) onion, sliced into thin rings
1 beef bouillon cube
1 medium green pepper, cut in strips
3 tbs. (1 oz.) yellow cornmeal
1/2 tbs. olive or other oil

Mix beef with onion powder and form into a thin patty. Put meat on rack in broiler

138

pan and broil on each side until fat has dripped out but meat is still moist. Put meat in a 4-cup baking dish and immediately crumble with fork; stir in tomato sauce, chili powder, garlic and salt to taste. Top with onion rings; reserve. Into small saucepan, put bouillon cube and 1 cup plus 2 tablespoons water. Bring to a boil, drop in green pepper just long enough to cook tender-crisp and remove with slotted spoon; put pepper on top of onions in casserole. Reduce heat so that remaining bouillon solution simmers and gradually pour in cornmeal, stirring constantly; cook until quite thick. Spread cornmeal mixture evenly across top of casserole, sealing edges. Bake at 350°F. for 20-30 minutes, or until bubbly and lightly browned on top. Drizzle on oil. Serve hot. Makes 2 servings.

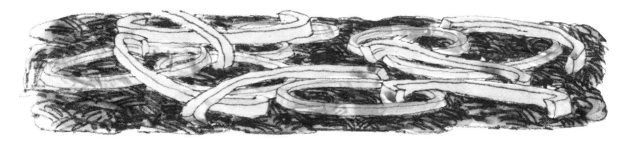

Calories: 460 per serving

VEAL PAUPIETTES

Lean veal is pounded very thin and rolled around minced mushroom stuffing.

1-1/3 cups (4 ozs.) chopped fresh mushrooms or
    1/2 cup (4 ozs.) minced canned mushrooms, drained
8 ozs. veal, thinly sliced as for scallopini
2 tsp. chicken seasoning (see page 6)
1 slice white bread, toasted, dried and blended into fine crumbs
1 tsp. minced parsley or 1/2 tsp. dried parsley
1/4 tsp. garlic powder
salt and freshly ground pepper
ground or crumbled thyme
1/2 small (2 ozs.) onion, chopped
1 medium (2 ozs.) carrot, diced
1/2 tsp. sherry or wine flavoring (optional)
1 or 2 tsp. butter or margarine

    If fresh mushrooms are used, simmer covered with 2 tablespoons water and 1/4 teaspoon salt for 7 minutes; drain and reserve. With meat mallet, pound cutlets on both sides until very thin (placing between waxed paper makes this easier). Combine cooked mushrooms, 1 teaspoon chicken seasoning, crumbs, parsley, garlic, salt and pepper. Divide and spoon mushroom mixture onto center of cutlets and roll each tightly; tie with white cotton string. Sprinkle each roll delicately with thyme. In a nonstick skillet over medium-high heat, brown rolls by adding remaining chicken seasoning and just enough water to form a coating in which the rolls can be turned. Then add 1/2 cup water, onion and carrot. Cover and barely simmer for 30 minutes, or just until most of the liquid is gone (add more water a spoonful at a time if necessary). Pour sherry flavoring over rolls, cover and simmer a minute longer. Arrange rolls on serving platter, pour on pan juices with vegetables and dot rolls with butter. Makes 2 servings.

Calories: 360 per serving

VEAL PARMIGIANA

Veal may be expensive, but it is the leanest of meats and therefore a good buy for those also striving to be lean.

3 ozs. veal, sliced very thin as for scallopini
1 tsp. chicken seasoning (see page 6)
1/4 tsp. onion powder
salt
1/3 cup tomato sauce
1 tbs. minced parsley or 1 tsp. dried parsley
1/4-1/2 tsp. garlic powder

1/4 tsp. each crumbled
    rosemary and oregano
freshly ground pepper
3 tbs. (1/2 oz.) imported mozzarella
    or Swiss cheese
2 tbs. (1/2 oz.) grated Parmesan cheese
2 tsp. olive oil

With meat mallet, pound veal on both sides until thin and light. Sprinkle both sides lightly with chicken seasoning, onion powder and salt. Place in a shallow baking dish in a single layer. Combine tomato sauce, parsley, garlic powder, rosemary, oregano and pepper. Spread half over meat and top with mozzarella cheese. Spread remaining sauce mixture over cheese. Sprinkle with Parmesan. Bake at 350°F. for 20-25 minutes. Drizzle on oil. Makes 1 serving.

Calories: 360 per serving

BLANQUETTE DE VEAU

A creamy veal stew.

about 7 ozs. boneless lean veal, cut in cubes
1 tsp. chicken seasoning (see page 6)
1/2 medium onion (2 ozs.), sliced in thin rings
1/3 cup (2 ozs.) carrot, thinly sliced
bouquet garni of 1 bay leaf, 3 whole cloves and 5 whole black peppers tied in cheesecloth
2 cloves garlic, minced
1 cup sliced fresh mushrooms or 1/3 cup sliced canned mushrooms
salt and freshly ground pepper
1 slice white bread
pinch nutmeg
1/2 cup nonfat milk
1/2 tsp. sherry or wine flavoring (optional)
1 tsp. lemon juice
2 tsp. butter or margarine

144

In nonstick skillet over medium-high heat, sear and lightly brown veal by sprinkling on chicken seasoning and just enough water to coat meat as you turn it. Add onion, carrot, bouquet garni and garlic. Cover with water, cover pan and simmer for 1 hour. Add mushrooms, salt and pepper; simmer covered about 1 hour more, or until liquid is reduced to about 1/2 cup. Drain liquid into blender jar, add bread torn in pieces and nutmeg; blend until smooth. Add milk and blend again. Pour into small skillet over medium heat and cook, stirring, until thickened. Add sherry flavoring, lemon juice and more salt and pepper if needed. Pour over veal. Drizzle butter on servings. Makes 2 servings.

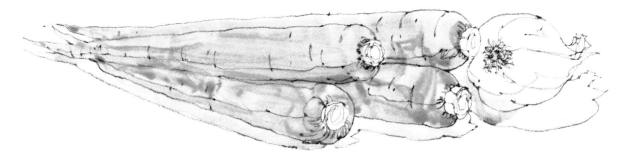

Calories: 310 per serving

OSSO BUCO Italy

An earthy, filling stew from the Lombard district of Italy. A good dish to expand.

8 ozs. veal shank or shoulder blade
1 tsp. chicken seasoning (see page 6)
1/2 medium onion (2 ozs.), thinly sliced
1/3 cup (2 ozs.) carrot, finely chopped
1 stalk celery, minced
2 tsp. minced parsley
oregano

2 cloves garlic, minced
1 bay leaf
salt and freshly ground pepper
1 cup tomato juice
1 tsp. grated lemon peel
1/2 tsp. sherry flavoring (optional)
2 tsp. olive oil

In a nonstick skillet over medium-high heat, brown veal by sprinkling with the chicken seasoning. Add just enough water to coat meat with the seasoning as you turn it. Top with onion, carrot, celery, parsley, oregano, garlic and bay leaf. Season with salt and pepper. Pour tomato juice gradually over so as not to disturb vegetables. Cover and simmer for about 1-1/4 hours, adding water if necessary. The dish is done when the meat eases off bones and a thick puree has formed. Add grated lemon peel and sherry flavoring. Drizzle on oil. Makes 1 serving.

Calories: 410 per serving

YOGUBAB

The full Turkish name of this kebab with yogurt sauce is Yogurtlu Kofte Kebab. Modern Turkish cooks use relatively few spices. But in the old days of the sultans a palace chef would have added the many seasonings this version contains.

8 ozs. ground lean lamb
1 tsp. (or less) ground cumin
1/2 tsp. ground coriander
1/4 tsp. each tumeric and ground cardamom
several dashes cinnamon

salt and freshly ground pepper
3 or 4 cloves garlic, minced
1 beef bouillon cube
3/4 cup yogurt
2 tsp. olive oil

Mix lamb with all the spices plus salt and pepper. Form into small meatballs and arrange on rack in broiler pan. Broil 6 inches below heat turning until browned but still very moist. In skillet, combine 1/4 cup water, garlic and bouillon. Bring to a boil, add meatballs, lower heat to simmer and cook until water is absorbed, about 12-15 minutes. Cool slightly; add yogurt. Heat, stirring, just until hot (do not let boil or sauce will curdle). Drizzle oil over servings. Makes 2 servings.

LULEH KEBAB

Spiced meatballs and vegetables on a skewer, topped with an exotically seasoned sauce. Indulge in a half cup of rice with this dish. Delicious.

8 ozs. ground lean lamb
1/4 tsp. each onion powder, ground cumin and cinnamon
1/2 tsp. crumbled mint leaves
salt and freshly ground pepper
1 medium firm tomato, cut in chunks
1 medium green pepper, cut in pieces
1/2 cup buttermilk
1 beef bouillon cube
1/4 tsp. each crumbled mint leaves and ground coriander
1/2 tsp. minced parsley or 1/4 tsp. dried parsley
lemon juice

In bowl, mix lamb, onion powder, cumin, cinnamon, mint leaves, salt and pepper. Form into 9 meatballs. Use short metal or wooden skewers (soak wooden ones in water so

148

they won't burn). Thread 3 meatballs on each skewer with tomato and pepper in between. Place on rack in broiler pan and broil 6 inches below heat until lamb is brown outside and no longer pink inside. Meanwhile, prepare sauce: in small skillet, combine remaing ingredients. Heat but do not let boil in order to prevent curdling. Pour over skewers. Makes 1 serving.

Calories: 560 per serving

MOUSSAKA

Greece

This eggplant casserole can be made in quantity to serve guests. It's a good party dish because it can be baked ahead of time and reheated at the last minute.

2 small eggplants
salt
8 ozs. ground lean lamb
1 tsp. chicken seasoning
1/4 tsp. onion powder
2 cloves garlic, minced
about 2/3 cup tomato sauce
1 tbs. minced parsley or 1 tsp. dried parsley

1/4 tsp. sherry or wine flavoring (optinal)
1/8 tsp. cinnamon
nutmeg
freshly ground pepper
1 slice white bread
1/2 cup nonfat milk
1 tbs. Parmesan cheese
1 tsp. olive oil

Cut eggplants lengthwise into thin slices. Sprinkle both sides lightly with salt and lay on paper towels (this causes water and bitter flavor to come out of eggplant). Drop slices in boiling water and cook until barely tender. Dry on paper towels. Meanwhile, mix lamb with chicken seasoning, onion powder and garlic. Form into a thin patty and place on rack in broiler pan. Broil on both sides until fat is rendered but meat is still moist. In bowl, crum-

150

ble meat finely with a fork and add 1/3 cup of the tomato sauce, parsley, sherry flavoring, cinnamon, a pinch of nutmeg, salt and pepper to taste. In 9-inch square baking pan, make a layer of half the eggplant, spread lamb mixture on top and add remaining eggplant. Pour the rest of the tomato sauce on top. Make sauce: To blender jar, add bread torn in pieces, milk and a pinch of nutmeg; blend until smooth. Pour into small skillet over medium-high heat and cook, stirring, until thickened. Pour sauce over moussaka. Sprinkle delicately with Parmesan and bake at 350^{0}F. for 20-30 minutes, or until hot and browned. Drizzle oil on servings. Makes 2 servings.

Calories: 375 per serving

ONIONS STUFFED WITH LAMB

The stuffing would be good in green peppers as well.

1 lb. ground lean lamb (leg or loin)
1/2 tsp. onion powder
1/4 tsp. ground cumin
1/8 tsp. ground coriander
1 tbs. minced parsley or 1 tsp. dried parsley
1/4 tsp. crumbled basil

pinch each of oregano and thyme
2 cloves garlic, minced
salt and freshly ground pepper
1/4 cup tomato sauce
6 large onions
cinnamon

Mix lamb with spices, herbs, garlic, salt and pepper. Form 2 thin patties and put on rack in broiler pan. Broil on both sides until fat has dripped out but meat is still moist. Crumble with fork and mix with tomato sauce. Cut tops off onions; reserve. Remove enough of the insides to make a thick shell for stuffing (save insides for other use). Stuff shells with lamb mixture; pack tightly or stuffing will come out during baking. Put onion tops on, dust lightly with cinnamon and arrange in a close-fitting baking dish; add about 1/2 inch very hot water. Bake at 400°F. for 20-25 minutes, or until onion is tender and top is brown. Baste often with pan juices. Cool slightly and serve warm. Makes 3 servings.

Calories: 410 per serving

STUFFED CABBAGE ROLLS

No one will believe you count calories when you serve this kind of hearty fare.

1 medium head cabbage
8 ozs. ground lean lamb
1/4 tsp. onion powder
2 tsp. minced mint leaves or 1 tsp. dried mint
1/4 tsp. each cinnamon and ground cumin
2 cloves garlic, minced
1 firm tomato, finely chopped
1/2 cup cooked rice (see page 9)
1 cup tomato juice
1 tbs. lemon juice
1 beef bouillon cube
salt and freshly ground pepper

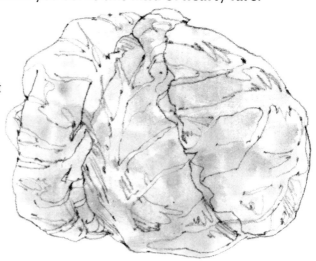

Remove and discard tough outer cabbage leaves; immerse head in boiling water until leaves come off easily; drain. Combine lamb, onion powder, half the mint, cinnamon,

154

cumin and half the garlic. Form into thin patty, put on rack in broiler pan and broil until fat has dripped out but meat is still moist. Crumble meat with a fork; mix in chopped tomato and rice. Make rolls with leaves as wrappers, using smaller leaves whole and trimming large ones to similar size: In center of each leaf, arrange a spoonful of lamb stuffing. Fold the side near you over filling, then fold sides over; roll up and fasten with a pick. In large skillet, arrange rolls side by side, touching. Pour in tomato and lemon juices; add bouillon cube, the remaining mint and garlic. Put a heavy plate on top of rolls to prevent unrolling. Cover skillet and simmer for 20 minutes, or until a thick sauce has formed. Serve hot. Makes 2 generous servings.

Calories: 320 per serving

PORK SATE

A spicy shish kebab to broil in oven or over charcoal.

1 lb. 12 ozs. boneless pork loin or rib, cut in 1-inch cubes
2 to 3 cups small (1 inch) mushrooms or larger cut in half
1 lb. small onions (walnut size)
1 cup soy sauce
1 tsp. garlic powder
1 tsp. turmeric or curry powder
freshly ground pepper
2 tbs. imitation mayonnaise
1 cup canned garbanzos, drained (save liquid)
2 tbs. brown sugar
1 tbs. sesame oil or peanut butter
1 tsp. walnut or peanut flavoring (optional)
salt and hot pepper sauce

In bowl, combine pork, mushrooms and onions. In saucepan, combine soy sauce,

156

garlic, turmeric and pepper. Bring to a boil and pour over the pork and vegetables. Marinate several hours or overnight in refrigerator, turning pieces occasionally. Make kebabs by alternating pork and vegetables on skewers (if wooden ones are used, soak in water first to prevent burning). Arrange on rack in broiler pan; broil 6 inches below broiler, basting occasionally with marinade; or charcoal broil. Be sure that pork is thoroughly cooked, no longer pink inside. But do not overcook or meat will toughen. To make sauce: Combine remaining ingredients in blender jar and blend until smooth, adding garbanzo juice as necessary. Heat in saucepan, pour over kebabs. Makes 6 servings.

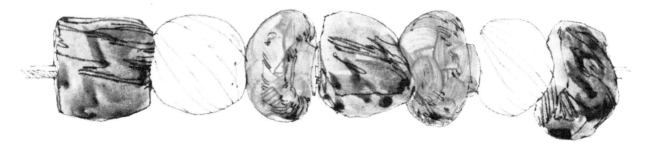

Calories: 460 per serving

MALAYSIAN KEBABS

Indonesia

This may well be the most delicious and beautiful way to enjoy liver. A food so low in calories and so high in nutrition.

8 ozs. chicken livers, cut in pieces
1/4 cup soy sauce
1/2 green pepper, cut in 1-inch pieces
1 cup small (1 inch) mushrooms or larger cut in half
1/2 cup unsweetened pineapple chunks plus 2 tbs. juice
1/8 tsp. turmeric or curry powder
1/8 tsp. ground ginger or 1 tsp. grated fresh ginger
1/4 tsp. garlic powder
freshly ground pepper
2 tsp. brown sugar

In nonstick skillet, fry liver in just a little of the soy sauce and enough water to make a glaze that aids browning; cook until firm but still pink inside. Make kebabs by alternating liver, green pepper, mushrooms and pineapple on skewers. If wooden ones are used, soak

them in water first to prevent burning. Arrange side by side in foil-lined broiler pan. Brush with remaining soy sauce and the pineapple juice. Sprinkle with turmeric, ginger, garlic and lots of pepper. Broil about 6 inches below heat for 5 minutes on each side, or until vegetables are tender and liver is no longer pink inside. Serve pan juices as sauce. Makes 2 servings.

Calories: 270 per serving

SWEET TREATS

There are so many choices to make when you are calorie counting. Questions like "Shall I skip a cocktail and have dessert instead?" seem to continually arise. Often you feel you must opt not to have dessert because of the high calorie count. You can enjoy desserts much more frequently when you use my recipes.

In the past, low calorie desserts were often loaded with sugar substitute. Their bitter taste gave lie to their enticing look. I use little sugar substitute and combine natural fruit flavors with it.

Desserts need not be the stumbling block that prevents you from succeeding in your weight control program. The craving for something sweet is natural for most of us. Cater to that urge sensibly with some of these ideas that allow you to stick to your diet.

BLANCMANGE WITH BERRIES

A simple sweet that turns any fresh fruit into dessert.

1 env. unflavored gelatin
2 cups nonfat milk
3 envs. sugar substitute
almond extract
2 cups sliced fresh strawberries, chilled

Soften gelatin in cold milk and pour into saucepan. Cook over low heat, stirring constantly, just until gelatin is dissolved. Remove from heat and stir in sugar substitute; add almond extract drop by drop, to taste. Pour into two 1-cup molds or a bowl. Chill until very firm. To serve, dip mold in warm water and unmold onto serving plate; surround with berries. Eat very cold. Makes 2 servings.

Calories: 165 per serving

COFFEE CUSTARD

If you can find a specialty store that sells mocha flavoring (essence of chocolate and coffee combined), you can make this dessert even more delicious without adding to its calorie count.

2 eggs
1-1/2 cups nonfat milk
2 envs. sugar substitute
2 tsp. instant coffee powder
mocha flavoring (optional)

Into blender jar, put eggs, milk, sugar substitute and coffee powder; blend at low speed. Add mocha flavoring to taste (start with about 1/2 teaspoon—as much as 2 teaspoons may suit you). Pour mixture into 3 custard cups, put in baking pan and add 1 inch very hot water. Bake at 350^{0}F. for 25-30 minutes, or until center is no longer liquid when pressed. Immediately remove from pan and cool. Eat warm or chilled. Makes 3 servings.

Calories: 147 per serving

ZABAGLIONE MOUSSE

This recipe stretches a few calories incredibly far. The cooking technique is unusual, but easy if you read the instructions and get the two ordinary pans arranged before beating the eggs.

2 large eggs, separated
2 envs. sugar substitute
1 cup diet carbonated cream soda, at room temperature
2 tsp. rum flavoring

For cooking the eggs, improvise a sort of double boiler. The arrangement differs from a double boiler in that the top pan sits down in simmering water, not above it: For the bottom pan use a 10-inch skillet; add about 2 cups water. Set another smaller skillet or wide, shallow saucepan in the water (you will cook the zabaglione in this pan). At serving time: In a bowl, beat egg whites until stiff. In another bowl, beat yolks with sugar substitute until they are pale yellow and light. Remove smaller pan from water and to it add the yolks, soda and rum flavoring. Heat the water in the skillet until it simmers; keep just at the simmering stage. Put pan with egg-soda mixture in water and beat at high speed until mixture becomes frothy and somewhat firm, like a mousse (this may take 10 minutes or more, depending on the heat). Remove from heat and immediately fold in egg whites; quickly pour into 2 parfait glasses or goblets. Eat while warm or chill. Makes 2 servings.

Calories: 80 per serving

CREAMY PEACH MOLD

I like this with peaches, but you may want to try it with apricots, nectarine, papaya or banana.

1 medium to large very ripe peach, peeled and mashed
1 tbs. (1 oz.) uncooked cream of rice cereal
tiny pinch of salt
1 or 2 envs. sugar substitute
1/2 tsp. peach flavoring (optional)
pinch of mace

In small skillet, combine peach with 3/4 cup water. Bring to a boil and gradually sprinkle in cereal in a steady stream, stirring constantly; cook for 2 minutes, or until thick and smooth. Remove from heat and quickly stir in remaining ingredients. Cover and let stand 5 minutes. Stir and pour into two 1-cup molds or small bowl. Chill until firm, about 20 minutes. Unmold by dipping mold into warm water. Eat at once. Makes 2 servings.

Calories: 78 per serving

APPLE CAKE

This is another of my sweet treats that is good for either dessert or breakfast.

4 medium apples, cored
4 large eggs
4 slices white bread, toasted
3/4 tsp. baking soda
1/8 tsp. cream of tartar

4 envs. sugar substitute
almond extract
1/4 cup butter or margarine
cinnamon

Cut apples in half horizontally (through sides, not stem ends). In 10-inch skillet, arrange halves side by side, cut sides up, and add 1/2 inch water. Cover and simmer 8 minutes, or until apples are softened but still hold their shape. With slotted spoon, carefully remove apples, drain and arrange in a 9-inch pie pan (apples should touch). Meanwhile, in blender jar, combine eggs, bread torn in pieces, soda, cream of tartar and sugar substitute; blend until smooth. Add almond extract to taste, starting with about 1/4 teaspoon. Pour batter over and between apples. Bake uncovered at 350^{0}F. for 20 minutes, or until browned and cake-like. Remove and, while hot, spread evenly with butter; sprinkle lightly with cinnamon. Eat warm or cold. Cut into 6 wedges.

Calories: 241 per serving

CRUSTY APPLE PIE

A pie with a dual purpose: breakfast or dessert.

6 medium apples, peeled,
    cored and thinly sliced
2 cups nonfat milk or 1 cup evaporated
    nonfat milk diluted with 1 cup water
3/4 cup ricotta or cottage cheese

3 large eggs
5 or 6 envs. sugar substitute
2 tsp. vanilla extract
1 tsp. cinnamon
1 cup instant nonfat dry milk

Arrange apple slices attractively in a 9-inch pie pan, overlapping in a circular fashion. Bake uncovered in a 350°F. oven for 20-30 minutes, or until apples become slightly soft. Meanwhile, in blender jar, combine 1 cup of the liquid milk, cheese, eggs, sugar substitute and vanilla. By hand stir in the remaining 1 cup liquid milk and cinnamon to taste. Pour blender mixture very gradually over apples to keep from disturbing arrangement. Sprinkle milk powder evenly across top and dust with cinnamon. Bake uncovered 30-35 minutes, or until browned and custard-like center no longer is liquid when pressed. Serve warm, at room temperature or chilled. Makes 6 servings.

Calories: 230 per serving

CLAFOUTI AUX PECHES

If you call this by its French name, this peach custard cobbler seems to taste even more extravagantly rich than it is.

6 medium, ripe peaches, peeled and sliced
7 slices white bread, crusts removed
2 cups nonfat milk
3 large eggs

nutmeg or mace
6 envs. sugar substitute
peach flavoring (optional)
almond extract

Arrange peaches attractively in a 9-inch pie pan, overlapping slices in a circular fashion. Heat oven to 350°F. To blender jar, add bread torn in pieces, milk, eggs, pinch of nutmeg, and sugar substitute; blend until smooth. Add flavoring and extract to taste (start with about 1/4 teaspoon of each). Pour batter gradually over peaches to avoid disturbing arrangement. Bake for 30-35 minutes, or until custard center no longer is liquid when pressed. Remove and cool. Serve lukewarm or chilled. Just before serving, sprinkle delicately with more nutmeg. Makes 6 servings.

EAT THE WHOLE PIE

Have you ever wanted to eat a whole pie? Here is a pie for you to eat alone when a ravenous mood strikes, or share with another, if you don't feel greedy.

1/2 cup evaporated nonfat milk
1 env. unflavored gelatin
2 envs. sugar substitute
1 tsp. grated lemon peel
2/3 cup ricotta or cottage cheese
1/4 cup yogurt or buttermilk
1 tbs. lemon juice
tiny pinch of salt

Cherry Topping:
1/2 env. unflavored gelatin
3/4 cup diet cherry-flavored carbonated beverage
1/2 tsp. cherry flavoring (optional)
1 env. sugar substitute
1/2 cup frozen pitted cherries, thawed

Put milk in mixing bowl and set in freezer until crystals begin to form (about 45 minutes). Meanwhile, into saucepan, put 1/2 cup cold water and the 1 envelope gelatin; soften gelatin and then cook on low heat, stirring, just until gelatin dissolves. Remove; add sugar substitute and lemon peel; cool at room temperature while you prepare cheese: In bowl, combine cheese, yogurt, lemon juice and salt; beat with rotary mixer until smooth.

Blend cheese mixture with gelatin mixture; chill, stirring occasionally, until it mounds slightly (do not let it gel). As soon as milk in freezer has formed crystals, beat with clean beaters until stiff like whipped cream. Beat in partially gelled cheese mixture, just enough to blend. Pour into 6-8 inch pie plate and chill until set. Meanwhile, make cherry topping: In saucepan, soften the 1/2 envelope gelatin in the cherry beverage. Cook over low heat, stirring, just until gelatin dissolves. Remove and blend in cherry flavoring and sugar substitute; cool. Drain cherries and fold in. Chill topping just until it mounds slightly but has not gelled. Spread over pie and chill further until all is firm, about 15-20 minutes. Eat the Whole Pie! Makes 1 or 2 servings.

Calories: 383 or 192 per serving

CHEESECAKE WITH GRAPES

Torta di Ricotta is a springtime tradition in Italy.

4 large eggs, separated
1-1/3 cups ricotta or cottage cheese
1 cup instant nonfat dry milk
5 envs. sugar substitute
freshly grated peel of 1 lemon and 1 orange

1 cup finely chopped seedless green grapes
1/2 cup yogurt or buttermilk
1 tbs. vanilla extract
3 cups whole grapes for garnish

In bowl, beat egg whites with rotary beater until very stiff peaks form. In another bowl combine egg yolks, cheese, milk powder, sugar substitute, grated citrus peels and chopped grapes; whip with beater until smooth. Blend in yogurt and vanilla, then gently fold in egg whites evenly. Pour into 9-inch nonstick cake pan or square pan. Bake at 400°F. for 20-25 minutes, or just until center has firmed. Cool somewhat and turn out onto serving platter; surround with whole grapes. Eat at room temperature or chilled. (Or chill before turning out of pan.) Makes 6 servings.

Calories: 210 per serving

SKILLET STRAWBERRY SOUFFLE

Whether you call it a skillet souffle or a puffy omelet, this dish is easy and difficult—easy to make, difficult to resist.

1 cup sliced strawberries
1/8 tsp. almond flavoring
1-1/2 envs. sugar substitute
2 large eggs, separated

2 tsp. arrowroot or cornstarch
1/3 cup instant nonfat dry milk
1 to 2 tsp. rum flavoring
1 tsp. butter or margarine

In bowl, mix strawberries with almond flavoring and 1/2 envelope sugar substitute; reserve. Have ready a 10-inch nonstick skillet and lid; turn stove burner to low. In bowl, beat egg whites until they form very stiff, moist peaks, adding arrowroot gradually while you beat. Quickly beat in milk powder, the remaining 1 envelope sugar substitute, rum flavoring and egg yolks. Put skillet on burner and, when warm, pour egg mixture evenly in pan. Cover for 2 minutes and check for doneness: mixture should be cooked on outside but slightly runny on the inside. Distribute strawberries along center, fold over and slide onto serving plate. Dot with butter. Eat at once. Makes 1 large or 2 small servings.

Calories: 300 or 150 per serving

BANANA BREAKFAST SOUFFLE

Conventional breakfast foods converted to something special. Notice how low that calorie count is, too.

2 slices white bread
1 cup evaporated nonfat milk
nutmeg
3 envs. sugar substitute
4 very ripe medium bananas
4 large eggs, separated
1/4 to 1/2 tsp. each coconut and banana flavoring (optional)

In blender jar, combine bread torn in pieces, milk and pinch nutmeg; blend until smooth. Pour into small skillet; over low heat gradually bring to simmer and cook, stirring constantly, until thickened. Remove, stir in sugar substitute and pour into bowl. Slice bananas into blender jar and add egg yolks; blend until smooth. Mix banana mixture into bread-milk mixture; reserve. Stir in flavorings to taste. In another bowl, beat egg whites until they form stiff but moist peaks. Fold whites into banana-milk mixture and pour into 4-6 cup souffle dish. Bake at 375^0F. for 25-30 minutes, or until center is no longer liquid when pressed. Sprinkle with nutmeg, if you like. Makes 4 servings.

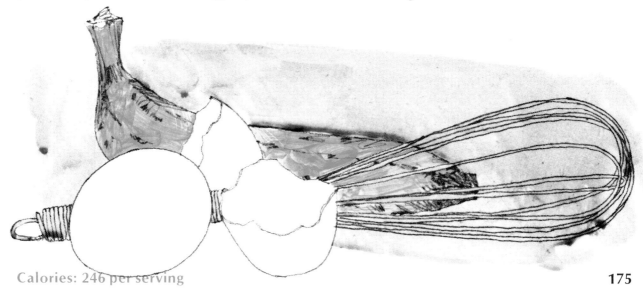

Calories: 246 per serving

BLUEBERRY CREPE

I make this often for family breakfast because it is my daughter Tania's super favorite.

1/2 cup fresh or frozen blueberries
1 tsp. vanilla extract
2 env. sugar substitute
1 large egg

1/4 cup yogurt or buttermilk
1 slice white bread
ground cardamom (optional)
1 tsp. butter or margarine

Into saucepan, put blueberries, vanilla and 1 envelope of the sugar substitute; barely cover with water. Over medium heat, bring to a bubble and cook uncovered, stirring often, until the consistency of preserves. Remove from heat, cover and keep warm while you make the crepe. In blender jar, combine egg, yogurt, bread torn in pieces and the other envelope sugar substitute; blend until smooth. Add up to 1/4 teaspoon cardamom to taste. Heat 10-inch nonstick skillet over low heat and pour in blender contents, tilting pan to spread evenly. Lift edge with rubber spatula; turn only when brown-flecked or pancake may tear. Cook other side, then spread fruit in center and roll up. Serve dotted with butter. Makes 1 serving.

Calories: 265

BLUEBERRY BRAN MUFFINS

U.S.A.

1 large egg
1 tbs. buttermilk
1 tsp. vanilla extract
2 tbs. (1 oz.) 100% bran cereal
1/3 cup instant nonfat dry milk
1 or 2 envs. sugar substitute

1/4 tsp. baking soda
cream of tartar
cinnamon
1/2 cup small fresh or frozen blueberries
or minced cherries, drained
1 tbs. butter or margarine

Heat oven to 400°F. In blender jar, combine egg, buttermilk, vanilla, cereal, milk powder, 1 envelope of the sugar substitute, baking soda and a pinch of cream of tartar. Blend until smooth; taste and add another envelope sugar substitute and cinnamon (start with 1/4 teaspoon, then taste). With rubber spatula, fold blueberries evenly into batter. Pour into nonstick muffin pan (recipe should half fill 6 cups). Bake for 12-15 minutes, or until puffed and golden brown. Spread with butter. Eat warm. Makes 6 muffins.

Calories: 53 per muffin

BANANA CORN MUFFINS

Each muffin has fewer calories than a slice of plain bread.

3 tbs. (1 oz.) yellow cornmeal
1 large egg
1/3 cup instant nonfat dry milk
1/4 tsp. baking soda
pinch of cream of tartar
ground ginger
1/4 tsp. coconut flavoring or vanilla extract
1 env. sugar substitute
1 medium banana
2 tsp. butter or margarine

Heat oven to 400°F. In blender jar, combine all ingredients except banana and butter. Blend until smooth. Mash banana with fork or chop in small chunks. Stir into batter, then pour into nonstick muffin pan (batter should half fill 6 cups). Bake 12-15 minutes, or until golden and puffed. Spread on butter. Eat warm. Makes 6 muffins.

Calories: 63 per muffin

INDEX